The Forbidden Modern

Critical Perspectives on Women and Gender

Critical Perspectives on Women and Gender brings books on timely issues and controversies to an interdisciplinary audience. The series explores gender-related topics and illuminates the issues involved in current debates in feminist scholarship and across the disciplines.

Titles in the series

Michelle Fine
Disruptive Voices: The Possibilities of Feminist Research

Susan D. Clayton and Faye J. Crosby
Justice, Gender, and Affirmative Action

Janice Doane and Devon Hodges
From Klein to Kristeva: Psychoanalytic Feminism and the Search for the "Good Enough" Mother

Jill Dolan
Presence and Desire: Essays on Gender, Sexuality, Performance

Judith Newton
Starting Over: Feminism and the Politics of Cultural Critique

Jill G. Morawski
Practicing Feminisms, Reconstructing Psychology: Notes on a Liminal Science

Mary S. Gossy
Freudian Slips: Woman, Writing, the Foreign Tongue

Teresa L. Ebert
Ludic Feminism and After: Postmodernism, Desire, and Labor in Late Capitalism

Nilüfer Göle
The Forbidden Modern: Civilization and Veiling

Aída Hurtado
The Color of Privilege: Three Blasphemies on Race and Feminism

The Forbidden Modern

Civilization and Veiling

Nilüfer Göle

Ann Arbor

THE UNIVERSITY OF MICHIGAN PRESS

2003   2002   2001   6   5   4   3

*A CIP catalog record for this book is available
from the British Library.*

Library of Congress Cataloging-in-Publication Data

Göle, Nilüfer, 1953–
        The forbidden modern : civilization and veiling / Nilüfer Göle.
            p.   cm. — (Critical perspectives on women and gender)
        Includes bibliographical references and index.
        ISBN 0-472-09630-3 (alk. paper). — ISBN 0-472-06630-7 (pbk. :
    alk. paper)
        1. Women—Turkey—Social conditions.   2. Muslim women—Turkey.
    3. Women in Islam—Turkey.   4. Purdah—Turkey.   5. Veils—Turkey.
    I. Title.   II. Series.
    HQ1726.7.G65   1996
    305.42'09561—dc20   96-18179
                                                                    CIP

To my grandmother, Zehra Bozer

Acknowledgments

The first stage of this study, the historical research, was realized in Paris in 1985 with the support of UNESCO. Wassyla Tamzali, as her name bespeaks, was the spiritual guide for this project, as she has been in other areas of my life. She redirected my attention to my own past and country. The second stage, the fieldwork, took place in Turkey in 1987. I am thankful to Pierre Kalfon, of UNESCO, who provided support and flexibility.

Jean-Pierre Thieck, who is no longer among us, and Vincent Duclerc were among the first readers of the original text in French. They made me believe that I had something to say. Ali Bayramoğlu and Nihal İncioğlu encouraged me to make a book out of it; they also discussed and commented on the Turkish version. I would not have had the courage to rewrite it for the U.S. audience without the catalytic role Müge Göçek played in my life. Knowing her means a gain in intellectual synergy and interpersonal harmony. During my sabbatical at the University of Michigan in 1994 I benefited greatly from the exchanges with both my colleagues and students, whose own preoccupations and comments made me turn toward new questions.

I am thankful to Hüseyin Tapınç for his assistance in the translation to English.

I miss Alain Touraine, whose personal curiosity, originality, and authority provided my intellectual frame during my ten years in Paris. My training continues in Turkey, in a frameless society open to all kinds of atypical practices. I am, above all, grateful to these Turkish actors, in particular to the Islamist women.

Absences for fieldwork, conferences, and a sabbatical; writing reports and articles; new research projects; new international workshops; the sound of the computer; piles of books and xeroxed articles; deadlines, panics, and postponed vacations. . . . I thank my husband, Asaf Savaş Akat, who helps to turn this mess into playfulness.

Contents

1. Introduction   1

2. Woman: The Touchstone of Westernization   27

3. Kemalism: The Civilizing Mission   57

4. Veiling: The Symbol of Islamization   83

5. Conclusion   131

   Notes   141

   Bibliography   161

   Index   169

CHAPTER 1

Introduction:
The Forbidden Modern

Veiling—that is, the wearing of a head covering and long, loose-fitting gowns—refers to the political reappropriation of Islamic religiosity and way of life rather than its trivialization within established tradition. Veiling is the most salient emblem and women the newest actors of contemporary Islamism.[1] No other symbol than the veil reconstructs with such force the "otherness" of Islam to the West. Women's bodies and sexuality reappear as a political site of difference and resistance to the homogenizing and egalitarian forces of Western modernity. The contemporary veiling of Muslim women underscores the insurmountability of boundaries between Islamic and Western civilization.[2] In other words, women's covered bodies reveal the centrality of the gender question and sexuality in Islamist critiques of Western modernity. Islamism brings forth women as markers of modesty and morality. By the same token women's participation and politicization engenders the formation of a public and collective identity for women that distances itself from definitions of separate gender roles within the domestic sphere. Hence, as a contemporary emblem for the Islamicization of a way of life and the politicization of religion, Islamic veiling cross-cuts power relations between Islam and the West, modernity and tradition, secularism and religion, as well as between men and women and women themselves.

This book explores the significance of the veiling movement in Turkey through a multilayered analysis of power relations ranging from the most private gender relations to the conflictual encounter between civilizations. Women's veiling is pursued as an analytic thread, one that interweaves the power relations concealed by the "civilizing process" between "East and West,"[3] one that knits the fabric of Islamism and illuminates the patterns of Western modernity through the prism of Islamism. Therefore, this is a study of the "embeddedness of gender"[4] in the elaboration of Islamism on the one hand and modernism on the other. I argue that contemporary

Islamism cannot be adequately understood in isolation from the local constructs of Western modernity in which women have an edificatory role.

This introductory chapter is a reassessment of the tensions between the theoretical and methodological trajectories of the book. The research project originated from an observable event—namely, the Islamist veiling movement of university students in Turkey during the post-1983 period. The issue of veiling became a decisive force in the radicalization of the Islamist movement once female students wearing headscarves were banned from universities, causing veiled students to mobilize, organizing sit-ins and demonstrations. Veiling can thus be considered as a social movement in that Muslim female students articulate their claims collectively and publicly and define the objectives of their action autonomously. The veiling movement has become a source of political conflict and polarization between secularists and Islamists, one that has engaged intellectuals, university faculty, mass media, and political parties in a fierce debate. But, foremost, this debate has revealed the deep social and cultural cleavages between secularists and Islamists in general and among women in particular. In a way it has revealed the extent to which "Westernist" versus "Islamist" confrontations have been reproduced among the citizens of the same nation, religion, and gender. This study also stems from the "personal uneasiness" of the author, both as a Turkish intellectual and woman. First, the most cherished master-narrative in Turkey relating education and modernization to woman's emancipation is contested by educated Islamist women. The premise that traditions and religion disappear with the advent of modernity, an evolutionary progression that is often taken as a natural consequence of secular scientific education, no longer holds. Second, as a product of Turkish secular modernism, I am puzzled by the advent of this new Islamic figure of women sharing the same classes, educations, and professions but asserting at the same time their aspirations for an Islamic ideal and identity; the commonality or communicability between these two figures of women, of the same religion, nationality and gender, thus becomes one of the questions underlying this study. Hence, I will attempt to establish a link between "private uneasiness" and "public issue," between "biography" and "history," thereby trying to translate my own experience into Mill's term, through a "sociological imagination."[5]

The first section of this chapter describes the sociological significance of the political debate about Islamist veiling. The second section discusses the methodological difficulties stemming from the shift in master-narratives to a focus on agency and meaning within a highly polarized and politicized context. These difficulties are not limited in time and space to the conditions of the research; instead, they lead to the more general question of the location of the researcher, to the connection between intellectuals and knowledge, culminating in the age-old social science problem of the connection between analysis and engagement, between structure and agency. The third section reviews the Turkish mode of modernization (initiated by the Ottoman-Turkish elites during the nineteenth century and resulting in the foundation of a secular nation-state by Mustafa Kemal Ataturk in 1923) in order to grasp from a historical perspective the contemporary dispute between Islamists and modernists. It reexamines the transformative impact of modernization on the private and public spheres, on the relations between men and women, and on the self-definition of Turks. It problematizes the cherished concept of "universal civilization" held by Turkish reformist elites, which came to be synonymous with Western European culture. The fourth section argues for the need to locate and study women as the symbols and central agents of this "civilizing project." The fifth section discusses the significance of Islamist movements, and more particularly that of Islamist veiling, in terms of the intrigue and resistance it offers to the civilizing project. It depicts the ways in which the Islamist identity, constructed in gendered terms, can not be separated from the perceptions and constructions of Western modernity. The sixth section studies Islamism's implicit critique of secular ways of life, one that results in women's corporal and public invisibility. Finally, the last section examines the conflicting agendas Islamist women acquire through participating in secular education and religious politics, on the one hand, and adhering to the principles of Islamist communalism, on the other. While the former necessitates public participation, the latter sanctions the individuation of women, whose morality specifically involves community and Islamist authenticity.

Sociological Significance of Veiling

Islamic veiling is a political issue in both Muslim and Western European countries: it highlights the tension within the core values of society, ranging from secularism of the public space, the place of religion in education, and individual rights to multiculturalism and multiconfessionalism.[6] The veiling of Islamist students appears as a controversial issue because it is the most visible reminder of religiosity and traditional roles of women in modern social contexts, such as university campuses, urban centers, political organizations, and industrial workplaces. This veiling is commonly perceived as a force of "obscurantism" and is often identified with women's subservience; as such, it is interpreted as blurring the clear-cut oppositions between religion and modernity and as an affront to contemporary notions of "gender emancipation" and "universal progress." Hence, the revival of Islamist movements throughout the Muslim world is often interpreted as a challenge to Western modernity, which is built upon a unidirectional notion of evolutionary progress conceived in terms of binary oppositions between religion and secularism, the private and public spheres, and particularism and universalism. Also Islamist veiling embodies the battleground for the two competing conceptions of self and society, Western and Islamist. Metaphorically, women's covered bodies revitalize contemporary Islamist movements and differentiate them from the secularist project.

I therefore argue here not only that the question of veiling is not an auxiliary issue for Islamist movements but, on the contrary, highlights the centrality of the gender issue to Islamist self-definition and implied Western criticism. Hence, veiling is a discursive symbol that is instrumental in conveying political meanings. Accordingly, the significance of contemporary Islamist movements can only be understood, I believe, in terms of their problematic relation to Western modernity, a relation that takes shape and acquires sense through women's bodies and women's voices. Islamism, therefore, is shaped by a selective reconstruction of identity rather than by an unchanging—that is, a historical and context-free, or fixed—identity. Consequently, it can be said that the questions of women, modesty, and sexuality are discerned and problematized by the contemporary Islamist movements more as a result of critical dependence on modernity rather than of loyalty to Islamic religion.

In its contemporary form veiling conveys a political statement of Islamism in general and an affirmation of Muslim women's identity in particular. In this respect it is distinct from the traditional Muslim woman's use of the headscarf.[7] While the latter is confined within the boundaries of traditions, handed down from generation to generation and passively adopted by women, the former is an active reappropriation by women that shifts from traditional to modern realms of life and conveys a political statement. Veiling is a political satement of women, an active reappropriation on their behalf of Islamic religiosity and way of life rather than its reproduction by established traditions. In this respect veiling does not express passive submission to prevalent community norms but, instead, affirms an active interest in Islamic scripture. Educated lower- and middle-class women claim to know the "true" Islam and hence differentiate themselves from traditional uneducated women; these young Islamist women reject foremost the model provided by their mothers, who are perpetuating traditions and traditional religion within their domestic lives without any claim to knowledge and praxis. Paradoxically, the veiled students, who owe their newly acquired class status and social recognition to their access to secular education, also empower themselves through their claim on Islamic knowledge and politics. Veiled students, as new female actors of Islamism, acquire and aspire for "symbolic capital"[8] of two different sources: religious and secular. Their recently acquired visibility, both on university campuses and within Islamist movements, indicates women's appropriation of this new symbolic capital and the emergence of a new figure, the female Islamist intellectual.

Furthermore, women's participation in Islamist movements symbolizes a new sense of belonging and ushers in a new community of believers. If the traditional way of covering oneself changes from one Muslim country to another in terms of the form of "folk" dresses, the contemporary Islamist outfit is similar in all Muslim countries: it is through the symbolism of women's veiling that a commonality of identity and the Muslim community (*umma*) is reconstructed and reinvented at the transnational level.

In sum, the veiling of women is not a smooth, gradual, continuous process growing out of tradition. On the contrary, it is the outcome of a new interpretation of Islamic religion by the recently urbanized and educated social groups who have broken away from traditional popular interpretations and practices and politicized religion as an assertion of their collective identity against modernity. The veiling of women is the most salient trait of the contemporary Islamist movement, which is grounded on this focal tension among Islamism, traditionalism, and modernism.

The difference between the two profiles of Muslim women and the new significance of veiling were sharply underlined by the "headscarf dispute," which erupted in 1984 in Turkey.[9] The use of the traditional headscarf by lower-middle-class women living on the fringes of modern city life has gone almost unnoticed, considered as a residual practice of traditionalism, while the adoption of the Islamist outfit by a group of university students, a phenomenon of the post-1983 period, is considered as a manipulative tool of the rising Islamist fundamentalist movement and, consequently, has provoked a very polarized political dispute between secularists and Islamists.

To distinguish the Islamist from the traditional way of covering, the Turkish mass media labeled the new veiling of women as the "turban movement."[10] The word *turban*, coined for the new veiling movement, is polysemic and hints at the transgressive nature of women's participation in Islamist movements. *Turban*, originally from Turkish *tül(i)bend* and Persian *dülband*, refers to a headdress of Muslim origin, consisting of a long linen, cotton, or silk scarf. In modern Turkish, however, it is employed as a French word, one denoting a fashion of headdress, itself adopted from Ottoman Turkish. As such, the word *turban* itself has witnessed the transmission, interplay, and interpenetration of words and practices between the Ottoman Turkish heritage and the West. Labeling the female Muslim students' movement of veiling as the "turban movement" differentiates it from use of the traditional headscarf and suggests fashion and a change— that is, a modern way of appropriation as opposed to simply perpetuating tradition. On the other hand, *turban* also means a religious garment used by men—that is, *sarık* in Turkish—and, though it recalls the power of Islamic *ulema* (religious classes), it is used to distinguish women's religious politicization and empowerment. Hence, the label "turban" itself reveals the hybrid and transgressive character of the Islamist veiling movement grounded on the power dynamics between East and West, traditionalism and modernity, men and women. Contrary to the traditional practice of Islamic veiling, or the Islamic headscarf, which conveys a specific meaning—that is—"return to traditions," "return to fundamentalism," "subservience of women"—and suggests binary oppositions such as "Islam is essentially different from the West," and "Westernization is a condition of women's emancipation," the label of "turban" represents the hybrid and transgressive nature of Islamism in general and women's participation in the Islamist movement in particular.

Agency, Conflictuality, and Self-Reflexivity

Theories of modernization have forced us to seek, and find, symmetrical and linear lines of development that occur almost independently of historical and geographical context. Today the epistemological pendulum is swinging from evolutionary reasoning and methodological positivism to the question of agency and the subsequent analysis of particularistic, context-bound interpretations of modernity and self. Such a shift has an undeniably liberating potential on the study of "non-Western" countries. The distancing from the universalistic master-narratives of modernization and emancipation opens up the space for the examination of subjective constructions of meanings, cultural identities, and social conflicts; in short, it enables the examination of the specific articulations between modernity and the local fabric.

The move toward new forms of interpenetration and hybridization between the particularistic and universalistic, the local and global, situates us on a terrain that is not designated, determined, and mediated by social scientific language. This new positioning leads to the common tendency of naming all sorts of puzzling hybridizations and paradoxes as either parochial signs of a "pathology of backwardness" or, on the other extreme, as culturalist essentialism[11] or simply as postmodern relativism. Hence, such a move brings with it a problem of conceptualization and necessitates new linkages between empirical and theoretical languages. It also necessitates a repositioning of the researcher with respect to "local" context and native language. The weakening of the master-narratives of modernization and emancipation changes the role of intellectuals from transmitters and defenders of universal values to that of interpreters of hybrid, paradoxical, multidirectional social realities.[12] This new attention can be translated into a sociological awareness only through the mediation of a context-bound language.

The original Turkish title of this book, *Modern Mahrem*, for instance, articulates the difficulties in crossing cultural boundaries and national languages: *Mahrem* literally refers to intimacy, domesticity, secrecy, women's space, what is forbidden to a foreigner's gaze; it also means a man's family. In the text the concept of "mahrem" illuminates the difficulty of rendering this "private" space, private in the modern Western sense. The concept becomes more than a simple question of translation, an analytic category, a key for understanding the issues of intimacy, sexual segregation, and communal morality in a Muslim society. Using the Western concept of "private sphere" instead of *mahrem* would have led to the suppression of the distinctiveness of the domestic sphere in a Muslim context. Understanding the particularities from within therefore requires a broad sociological consciousness and conceptualization.

Similarly, the word *modern* literally indicates the Western set of values of individualism, secularism, and equality produced by the Enlightenment, the industrial revolution, and pluralistic democracy; it does not have a synonym in Turkish.[13] But it does have its own life and meaning in Turkish history. Rather than *modernity*, which refers to a given consciousness of the present time and state of development, the concept of "modernization"— expressing a political will to "become modern"—is used in the Turkish vocabulary of history and politics. Modernization can be interpreted as a continuous endeavor to overcome the lag in scientific, economic, and political development. As a consequence, Western modernity as a construct is an intrinsic part of Turkish intellectual and political life that changes over time and according to the ideological climate. No accurate reading of history, social agency, and social conflict is possible without taking into consideration this dependence on the concept of modernity. Public narratives (e.g., about Westernization, progress, the emancipation of women) as well as counter-narratives of oppositional movements (e.g., leftism, Islamism) carry the imprint of a problematic relation to modernity. If we want to understand and account for practices of social actors, ontological narratives, collective identities, and political conflicts, we must first recognize that at the very level of individual and collective identities it is necessary to decode local constructs of modernity. In other words, modernity cannot be conceived as a geographical entity, external to the Turkish experience but, on the contrary, needs to be elaborated as part of the historical experience, social setting, and the identity of social actors. It is in non-Western settings that modernity needs to be examined for its part in shaping public narratives, collective identities, and social practices.

Thus, the title *Modern Mahrem* combines two distinct yet interpenetrating civilizational categories: one intimate, gendered, and secret and the other public, universalist, and manifest. It alludes to the unsolicited encounter and interaction between Islam and modernity throughout Turkish history and hints more particularly at the Islamist woman's critical assessment of modernity and her forbidden participation in the public sphere. This book highlights and interprets local constructions of self and modernity, hybrid conjunctions, and asymmetrical social realities as forms of social practice and not as deviations from the evolutionary trajectory predicted by modernization theories. On the contrary, discrepancies between social theories and social practices are taken as a starting point of inquiry instead of simply juxtaposing ready-made social scientific language with a given social phenomenon and thereby suppressing the particulars.

Typical social theories explain Islamist movements in general and veiling in particular by assigning priority either to sociopolitical factors or to the essence of the religion itself, presumed to be alien to a series of transformations, such as reformism and secularism, that took place in the West. The first stand leads to causal explanations in which economic stagnation, political authoritarianism, rural exodus, and urban anomie are enumerated as the causes of radical Islamism. Even though such approaches describe the social environment within which oppositional movements are rooted, they fail to explain how and why Islam acquires such an appeal for cultural and political empowerment. The approaches that give priority to the Islamic essence, on the other hand, suppose an immutable nature of Islam and therefore take the religion out of its historical and political context. In this perspective Islamism and Islamic veiling appear as a "deviation" or a "pathology"; the underlying assumption of the argument is that, if modernization and secularization were successful, such "anamolous reactions" would not occur. And for both the political as well as the cultural approaches, the veiled women are an extension of a wider phenomenon: either as subsidiary militants of the fundamentalist political movement or as passive transmitters of traditional values. Such analyses, giving priority to the determinism of the system and structure, ignore the questions of agency and the formation of an Islamic actor and their contribution to the (re)production of the Islamic social order.

Fortunately, recent social theories have focused increased attention on questions of agency and cultural reproduction. Within the perspective of the sociology of action, social movements are not explained as anomalies but, instead, as contributing to the "self-production of society."[14] Social movements express the struggle for the control of historicity, that is, for the control of a cultural model that is not distinct from social conflict, through which society produces and reproduces itself.[15] Therefore, focusing on the questions of agency and identity becomes integral to an understanding of how the society reproduces and also transforms itself.

Emphasizing the questions of agency and identity and locating women at the center of our analysis will lead to new perspectives in the understanding of the discord between Islamism and modernism as it opens up a new territory of conflict. As such, focusing on Islamist women will not be limited to an examination of women's narratives and practices but will be enlarged to gain an understanding of how women's agency (or lack of agency) acts upon Islamist social movements. The focus of this analysis will thus be situated at the interplay between gender identities and political ideologies, at the intersection of ideological configurations and everyday power relations between the sexes. As Michel Foucault puts it, the body is the locus of all struggles of power, which works by the organization and division of space. The analysis of power, not as established domination (as something people hold) but, rather, as a "set of open strategies," will enable us to investigate the significance of the veiling movement at the level of the subjectivity of social actors and their social practice.[16] Consequently, identities (Islamist and women's) are not taken as fixed, essentialist categories but as reconstructions over time as well as accommodations to power relations. Thus, the formation of a collective identity for Islamist women can only be elaborated upon in their relationships with secularist women, with Islamist men, and also with other Muslim women. Once the narratives of women are historicized and contextualized, the fixity of identities can be transcended.[17]

A rethinking of Islamist veiling in terms of agency requires a sociological approach and method that render narratives of social actors in terms of their relationships and conflicts. Therefore, the choice of the sociological method is not independent from the general sociological approach. Although both deep interviews and group discussions are used in this study, the latter are privileged to the extent that they provide a relational setting and reinforce the self-reflexivity of actors. The group discussions were conducted according to the principles of "sociological intervention," elaborated by Alain Touraine as a method of the sociology of action.[18] Discussions in groups render narratives of Islamist women within a relational setting—that is, both in relation to one another and to the sociologist but also in relation to adversaries or spokepersons of the movement invited to the group. For instance, the encounter of the group first with one of the powerful male Islamist intellectuals defending women's rights from within Islam, and a later one with a secularist, Westernized feminist differed radically in both the terms of the debate as well the self-definition of the group. Sociological intervention gives a chance to analyze the formation of a collective identity of women in its shifting boundaries, in its conflictuality, and in its accommodation to power relations. The group members meeting with one another, the sociologist, and the invited outsiders discover their differences and acquire a sense of "memory" and of "history." As the research situation creates a distancing from the imperatives of collective action and identity, it increases in turn the self-reflexivity of the actors, urging them to go beyond given opinions. Sociological intervention gives priority to the production of meaning and knowledge as an interactive process between the actors and the analyst. The label "intervention" recalls this need to interact with actors of the movement in order to produce meanings of narratives, agency, and conflictuality. In a sense there is a place for "surprise" built into a research process, making space for the agency and self-analysis of actors, which would engender unanticipated meanings and conflicts, requiring new conceptualizations in turn. In other words, in a research situation the researcher faces aspects of the studied subject matter that do not fit, which are dissonant or simply meaningless in the context of the theoretical framework developed beforehand. Disregarding these aspects can be disabling for the understanding of the social dynamics. Thus, at a given stage of the research process the "disempowerment" of the researcher—that is, recognition of the rigidity of the theoretical framework in respect to the experiential, thus malleable, empirical world—is necessary if new territory of the meaning of social action and history is to be explored.

To sum up, the trajectory of the sociological analysis presented here can be described as a move from an observable micro-level event (the headscarf dispute) to focused research (of veiled Islamist students), which in turn highlights the general problem of Islamism and modernism from the point of view of women. The book begins by giving the historical setting, although the historical analysis is not intended as an explanation of contemporary events. On the contrary, the contemporary discord between Islamists and modernists ushers in a new reading of history and a new reading of the Turkish mode of modernization, which in turn leads us to explore territories of exclusion and domination and to examine silenced representations of those stigmatized as "backward," "uncivilized," and "irrational"—that is, the "dark side" of modernization.

Weak Historicity and Western Modernity

Unlike Western modernity, which was forged by the forces of industrialization, production, and class conflict, Turkish modernization was an outcome of the Westernism and secularism of reformist elites for whom women's emancipation from the traditional Islamic way of life would pave the way to Westernization and secularization for the larger society. In almost all Muslim countries, due to the historical specificity of the mode of modernization, women's issues have been pivotal in constructing both Islamism and modernism.

The modernization project takes a very different turn in a non-Western context in that it imposes a political will to "Westernize" cultural codes, lifestyles, and gender identities. The terms *Westernization* and *Europeanization,* widely used by nineteenth- and twentieth-century reformers prior to the more recent emphasis on the structural and universal traits of modernization, overtly express the willingness to borrow institutions, ideas, and manners from the West. The history of Turkish modernization as almost a civilizational conversion can be considered a most radical example of such a cultural shift. In their attempts to penetrate the lifestyle, public manners, gender behavior, body care, and the daily customs of the people, as well as their willingness to change their self-conception as Turks, Kemalist reforms[19] extended far beyond the modernization of the state apparatus and the transition from a multiethnic Ottoman Empire to a secular republican nation-state. With the contemporary renewal of Islamist movements both in Turkey and elsewhere, it is crucial to return to history, to a reconsideration of this civilizational shift in order to understand the emotional, personal charge, *"habitus"* in Pierre Bourdieu's terms, which mark the realm of conflict between todays' Islamists and modernists.

As Western experience and culture basically define the terms of civilization, attempts at modernization in a Muslim country center around Westernization. Once Western history, from the Renaissance through the Enlightenment to industrialization and currently to the Information Age, became the terrain of innovation and the reference point of modernity, non-Western experiences faded and lost their power as world historymakers. Instead, these experiences have been defined as residuals, without specific names, viewed only in relation to the "West," as "non-Western," as "the rest," and, as today, as "Islamic," as "essentially" distinct from Western civilization. These non-Western societies which can no longer participate in the "carnival of change," are excluded from being bearers of history and knowledge; they are, instead, left on the periphery of Western civilization with a "mutilated outlook."[20] This exclusion in turn results in the formation of societies with "weak historicity," that is with a weak capacity to generate modernity as a societal "self-production," as an indigenous development grounded in the interaction of cultural fabric and social praxis. Weak historicity is the sociological counterpart of the economic definition of the developmental lag between the "core countries" and the "periphery" in terms of the level of economic production, cultural creativity, and scientific knowledge. Weak historicity represents the repercussions of this lag on the discursive constructs and praxis of social and political actors. In societies in which modernity does not emerge from the indigenous culture and its development, historymaking becomes a continuous effort toward modernization and Westernization (or later the refusal of it) shaped by the will of the society's political and intellectual elites.

The encounter of the East with the West has not produced a reciprocal exchange between the two cultures but, instead, has resulted in the decline of Islamic identity. The term *civilization* does not refer to the historical relativism of each culture, as in "Islamic," "Arabic" or "French" civilization, but, rather, designates the historical superiority of the West as the holder of modernity. The concept of "civilization" blankets many themes, ranging from technology and worldview to rules of decent manners to the provision of a conglomeration of the phenomena that make the West distinct from other contemporary yet "primitive" societies.[21] In other words, the concept of civilization is not a neutral, value-free concept; to the contrary, it specifies the superiority of the West and attributes universality to a specifically Western cultural model. In opposition to the German notion of "kultur," which stresses national differences, the concept civilization has a universal claim: it plays down the national differences, emphasizing instead what is imagined to be common among peoples.[22] More precisely, it expresses the self-image of the European upper class, who see themselves as the "standard-bearers of expanding civilization," thus serving as a counterpart to the other tendency in society, that of barbarism.[23] The concept of civilization encompasses the idea of progress, referring to something that is constantly in motion, moving forward. Not only does it solely designate a given state of development (of Western countries), but it also encapsulates an ideal to be reached (by the non-Western world). The ideology of positivism underlying the concept of civilization attributes universality to Western civilization and suggests its applicability at anywhere any time. Thus, the main objective of modernization, as Turkish modernists have stipulated perfectly well, is to "reach the level of contemporary civilization" (*muasır medeniyet seviyesine erişmek*), as defined by the West.

Civilizing "Kemalist" Women

The debate among Ottoman elites on the ways and limits of Westernization at the end of the nineteenth century reveals the significance of the unsettled link of modernization with cultural identity and, in turn, with gender. While the Ottoman Westernists argued that only the emancipation of woman from the religious constraints and traditional ties would bring on the civilizing process, the Ottoman conservatives conjectured that according such freedoms to women would inevitably lead to the breakdown of the moral fabric of society. Consequently, veiling, a sign of "backwardness" for the proponents of Westernization, because it implied the separation of women from "civilized human beings," became, on the contrary, a sign of "virtue" for conservatives protecting both women's sexuality and their social morality.[24] In this debate the Westernists eventually triumphed over the conservatives with the success of the Turkish Kemalist Revolution in 1923.

An exploration of the Islamic religion as a constituent element of a social organization based on the segregation of sexes is vital to understanding how and why the civilizing process of the Kemalist revolution was constituted and culturally coded in gendered terms. The most resistant antagonism between the Islamic and the modern Western civilizations can therefore be grounded in the normative definitions of gender relations, in the religious-cultural code of honor and modesty, and in the organization of interior and exterior spheres, as well as on the separation of male and female.[25] Unlike most national revolutions, which redefine the attributes of an "ideal man," the Kemalist revolution celebrated an "ideal woman." Within the emerging Kemalist paradigm,[26] women became bearers of Westernization and carriers of secularism, and actresses gave testimony to the dramatic shift of civilization.[27]

The grammar of Turkish modernization can best be grasped by the implied equation established between national progress and women's emancipation. More than the construction of citizenship and human rights, it is the construction of women as public citizens and women's rights that are the backbone of Kemalist reforms.[28] Kemalist reforms aiming at the public visibility of women and the social mixing of the sexes thus implied a radical change in the definitions of the private and public spheres and of Islamic morality based on female "modesty" and "invisibility." According to the Kemalist project, women's visibility and the social mixing of men and women thus endorse women's existence in the public sphere. The taking off of the veil by women (1924 onwards), the establishment of compensatory coeducation for girls and boys (1924), the granting of political rights such as eligibility for political offices, women's suffrage (1934), and, finally, the abolition of the "Sharia," the Islamic law, and the subsequent adoption of the Swiss Civil Code (1926) were all measures undertaken to guarantee the public visibility and citizenship of women in the new Turkish nation-state.

The celebration and acquisition of women's visibility both in their corporality and in their public roles as models for emulation thus made the secularization of social life in Turkey possible. Photographs of women unveiled, of women in athletic competitions, of female pilots and professionals, and photographs of men and women "miming" European lifestyles depicted the new modernist interpretations of a "prestigious" life in the Turkish nation-state.[29] Novels of the Turkish republic, focused on this new "civilized" way of life—on its decor, goods, and clothing—celebrated the ideal attributes and rituals of a "progressivist and civilized" republican individual: tea saloons, dinners, balls, and streets were defined as the public spaces for the socializing sexes; husbands and wives walking hand in hand, men and women shaking hands, dancing at balls, or dining together, reproduced the European mode of encounter between male and female. Among the cast of characters of the new republic, the serious, hard-working, professional women devoted to national progress, appeared as a touchstone set apart from a "superficial" and mannered claim for Euro-peanness.[30] Against Ottoman cosmopolitanism, Kemalist female characters endorsed seriousness, modesty, and devotion and accommodated the pre-sumed (preIslamic) Anatolian traditional traits—thus, they represented the nationalist project.

In summary, the civilizing process intruded upon Turkey, and other non-Western contexts, bringing with it new ethical and aesthetic values for self-definition, representations of the body, gender relations, lifestyles and spacial divisions; it labored in the minds and bodies through the establish-ment of education for women and their new corporal and public visibility; and it introduced the principles of equality and the social interaction of the sexes, two very problematic notions for Islamic social imagery and world. "Women's visibility, women's mobility, and women's voices"[31] were and continue literally and symbolically to form the stakes of the battle between the modernists and the Islamists in Turkey and elsewhere in the non-West-ern world.

"Islam Is Beautiful": The Quest for a New Distinction

The concept of civilization, once problematized, loses its value-free status and refers, instead, to the power relations between those who appropriate civilized manners and the "barbarian," "primitive" others. In the context of Turkish modernization the distinction between "civilized" and "uncivi-lized" manners has been highly scrutinized: the "*alla franca*" (European) mode and behavior are praised, whereas everything associated with the "*alla turca*" (Turkish) mode acquires a negative meaning. It is curious that Turks themselves currently label their own habits as if European eyes are watching over their daily lives and employ the foreign word *alaturka* to represent a sort of ideal self.[32]

The reappropriation of the term *alaturka* symbolizes that changes in lifestyles and aesthetic values are not innocuous, in that they reiterate the civilizational shift from an Islamic to a Western one, a shift in which taste, as a social marker, establishes cultural distinctions and social stratification among classes.[33] Hence, cultural codes and lifestyles define the stakes in the implicit power struggle between the Westernist and the parochial elites. Rather than employing the concept of social classes, which emphasizes economic exploitation for some, it is more useful to refer to this stratification through the concept of *habitus* that encompasses lifestyles.[34] One can argue that upper-middle-class Kemalist women, who acquire education and a professional career and who cultivate their bodies and ways of life in a "secular" manner, form a distinct social status group. Thus, the acquisition of social distinction and social status, rooted in the exclusion of the Islamic world, forms the main focus of social and political discord between the secularists and the Islamists. The Turkish experience can be considered unique among its Muslim counterparts in this "epistemological break," its radical discontinuity between traditional self-definitions and Western constructs. Although the majority of the Turkish population easily create hybrid forms to integrate their daily practice of religion, their traditional conservatism, and their aspirations to modernity, modernist elites, with their implicit value reference to binary oppositions, situate themselves squarely on the side of the "civilized," "emancipated," and "modern." Consequently, Kemalist women, liberated from the religious or cultural constraints of the intimate sphere and fully participating in public life, are faced with a radical choice: they can be either culturally Western or Muslim. It is this choice, and the polarity embedded within it, that generates cognitive dissonance around the separate value systems of the elites and the rest of the populace and thus raises the issue of competing legitimacies.[35] The subsequent discourse of the elites is formulated from the Kemalist center of power, fortified by state support against all "other" forms of opposition.

Contemporary Islamist ideology reveals this power struggle in an aggravated form by challenging the equation established by the modernist elites between "civilized" and "Westernized." It promotes the return of the Muslim actors to the historical scene in terms of their own religious morality. The Islamist body politic conveys a distinct sense of self (*nefs*) and society (*umma*), one in which the central issue becomes the control of sexuality through women's veiling and the segregation of the sexes in public life. Hence, the veiling of women emerges as the most visible symbol of this Islamization of the self and society. But, in addition, other social forms, such as beards worn by men and taboos regarding chastity, promiscuity, homosexuality, and alcohol consumption, define a new consciousness of the Islamic self and the Islamic way of life.

Thus, through the political radicalization of Islam, Muslim identity makes itself apparent and seeks to acquire legitimacy in a modern political idiom. Islamism emphasizes Muslim identity and reconstructs it in the modern world. Islamic faith and the Islamic way of life become a reference point for the re-ideologization of seemingly simple social issues such as the veiling of Muslim students at the university, allocation of prayer spaces in public buildings, construction of a mosque at the center of Istanbul, segregation of the sexes in the public transportation system, censorship of erotic art, and discouragement of alcohol consumption in restaurants. Activism regarding these issues demonstrates the Islamist problematization of a universalistic construction of Western civilization and criticism of the "secular way of life."

The problematization of social issues demonstrates that the Islamic movements share the same critical sensitivity with contemporary Western social movements vis-à-vis Enlightenment modernity. The Islamist movements are thus similar to civil rights, feminist, environmental, and ethnic movements[36] in that all display the force of the repressed identities and issues (race, gender, nature, ethnicity, and religion, respectively) when challenged by industrial modernity, and all reawaken latent memories and identity politics. Identity politics, particularism, and localism against the uniformity of abstract universalism are common features of the postmodern condition. In this regard, Islamism is similar to feminism. While feminism questions the universalistic and emancipatory claims of the category of "human being" and asserts, instead, women's difference, Islamism problematizes the universalism of the notion of civilization, and asserts Islamic difference. While women reinforce their identity by labeling themselves feminists, Muslims emphasize theirs by naming themselves Islamists. Civil rights activists also asserted the primacy of difference through the use of the motto "Black Is Beautiful," thus rejecting the equation of emancipation with *white* and *Western*. Difference, therefore, becomes the source of empowerment for contemporary social movements and the content of identity politics. It is in this context of the rejection of the universalism of Enlightenment modernity and the assertion of difference that the motto "Islam Is Beautiful" has gained credence among Muslims.

Islamist movements therefore render visible a realm of conflict, one whose terms are defined by different discursive constructs and normative values of self, gender relations, and lifestyles. It is situated at the crossroads of religion and politics. The self-definition of the Muslim subject acquires meaning only through the religious idiom, and radical politics empowers and conveys this meaning to society at large. This realm can be approached through Alain Touraine's analytical framework of the struggle for the control of historicity—that is, for a cultural model tied directly to class conflict.[37] In this formulation, Islamic movements do not solely express a reaction to a given situation of domination but also present both a countercultural model of modernization and a new paradigmatic self-definition.

Authenticity and Occidentalism

The quest for differentiation from the Westernized self, for an "authentic" Islamic way of life, has engendered a critical alertness for both traditional Islam and the contemporary forms of Western modernity imposed by the globalization of culture and lifestyles. Islamism conveys a tacit resistance to Western modernity and its four basic principles and forces of change: secularism, equality, individualism, and confessionalism. The most significant experiences of Western modernity (and the most alien to a Muslim context) are the expansion of secularization into new realms of life and the extension of the principle of equality into new social relations.[38] The principle of equality confers legitimacy on a continuous societal endeavor that aims to overcome all social differences that have been traditionally accepted as insurmountable and natural. As such, equality among citizens, races, nations, workers, and, last, the sexes defines the historical and progressive itinerary of Western societies. Similarly, as more realms of life are socially and historically reconstructed and delivered from transcendental natural definitions, the process of secularization deepens. This synergy between secularism and equality is the ultimate product of the modern Western individual, epitomizing his or her self-reflexivity as a mental and corporal being.

Another touchstone of differences between Westernized and Islamist individuals is in approaches to the human body. The semiotics of body care by the secularized individual and the religious one indicates asymmetric conceptions of the self and body. For the modern individual the body liberates itself progressively from the hold of natural and transcendental definitions and enters into the spiral of secularization; it penetrates that realm in which human rationality exercises its will to tame and master the human body through science and knowledge. Genetic engineering and biological reproduction are two examples of highly scientific interventions. Also, the phobia about cholesterol, taboos on smoking, and obsessions with fitness demonstrate how the word *healthy* has become magical in defining new lifestyles inspired by the scientific (rather than the erotic) desire of body cultivation. "Bodysculpting," fitness, svelteness, thinness, and cultivating energy emerge as the ideals of a modern individual witnessing the leveling of differences between the sexes (the interchangeability of roles and out-look) and ages (that all can be young forever), culminating in the replace-ment of lifecycles with lifestyles.[39] The Islamist discourse and practice, con-versely, scrupulously reinforces and creates hierarchies of the differences among sexes (e.g., veiling for women, beards for men) and among genera-tions (for women, e.g., the stages of virgin, married woman, then mother). Any blurring between the feminine and masculine roles, especially the physical masculinization of women, is considered a transgression. In this respect veiling is considered a trait of feminity, of feminine modesty and virtue. The conception of the body conveys a different set of meanings in which the body is transformed as it mediates devotion to religious sacra-ments and purified through religious practices such as ablutions, fasting, and praying. In addition to the physical body, the Islamic spiritual being (*nefs*) is mastered and purified through submission to a divine will. But, again, this comparison is not simply a matter of difference between the sec-ular and religious conceptions of self that could be valid for almost all reli-gions; instead, in this context it is a civilizational matter. The genealogy of self and body conceptions in the West and within Islam also helps explain the almost compulsory resistance of contemporary Islamists to secularism and equality. The Islamic self and community are reconstructed in opposi-tion to the premises of the modern individual; the Islamic identity searches for its "authenticity", and for its distinction from the Western identity in defining its essential foundational roots.[40]

Another distinctive drive of modern societies is the drive to "confess," to "tell the truth about sexuality," as Michel Foucault put it. According to Foucault, the emergence of modernity can only be understood within the context of this urge, which stems from earlier religious practices; it entails a desire to confess the most intimate experiences, desires, illnesses, uneasi-ness, and guilt in public in the presence of an authority who may judge, punish, forgive, or console the confessor.[41] This explains why everything rooted in the private sphere, long considered the most difficult to reveal, becomes public, political, and a source of knowledge once it is confessed. In a sense the motto of the feminist movement, "The Personal Is Political," contributes to this movement of exit from and transparency in the public sphere in that it focuses on the process through which intimate relations of domination are transformed into relations of power. Abortion rights, sexual harassment, and date rape witness, by the novelty of their labeling, this movement from the private to the public. Talk shows and popular trials have, for example, become a center of debate in U.S. society, mediating this urge to confess, to intrude on personal relations to detect the truth about the relations of power inherent in the private sphere.

While modern Western society reveals the truth about revelations in the private sphere, it also transforms truth into a matter of individual conscience.[42] In contrast to the interiorizing of truth in the modern West, Islam privileges the community (*cemaat*) in guiding the individual through life and giving oneself up to God. Veiling symbolizes the primacy of the community and conveys the forbidden, intimate sphere and the confinement of the self and sexuality within the limits of the private, thus shielding the private sphere from disclosure to the public gaze.[43]

The Islamic subject thus reveals him- or herself and quests for authenticity by refusing to assimilate into Western modernity and by rediscovering religion and memory, often repressed by Western secular rationalism and universalism. The reappropriation of Islam as a way of life provides a new anchor for the self and thereby recreates an "imagined political community"; it reinforces social ties among those individuals who do not know one another but who yearn for profound horizontal attachment.[44] Islamism works as an imagined community, one that is forged and reinforced by and within the realm of the sacred.[45] The Islamic way of life, as a selective construct of religion facing modernity, traces the borders of this imagined community and resists the trivialization of chosen lifestyles by the impact of the commodity logic and hedonistic individualism characteristic of modern times.

Woman's Personality or Islamic Communalism

The quest for difference and authenticity, though necessary for an initial elaboration of identity, nevertheless has its own limits. For instance, who decides such questions as What is really Islamic? and Who is a real Muslim? can lead to essentialist definitions and exclusionary standards, thereby turning the imagined community into an "oppressive communitarianism." The "return of the repressed" can in turn be repressive. This totalitarian tendency can be easily triggered by a search for the "total" Islamic identity, one freed from the "corrupt and dominating" effects of Western modernity. The more one reinforces the relationship between the "pure" self and "total" community, the more Islamic politics becomes an imposed lifestyle, veiling a compulsory emblem, and women the moral guardians of the Islamic identity and community. This would entail the control of the public sphere by means of canceling out individual choices in determining lifestyles, monopolizing the cultural code, and instituting an Islamist form of the colonization of the self.

In other words, the totalitarian dimension emerges from the utopian ideal of a single identity for the collectivity. The pairing of a fixed identity and a utopian community presupposes a harmonious, a historical nondifferentiated social order that avoids all subversive conflict. Women are the touchstones of this Islamic order in that they become, in their bodies and sexuality, a *trait d'union* between identity and community. This implies that the integrity of the Islamic community will be measured and reassured by women's politically regulated and confined modesty and identity (such as compulsory veiling, restricted public visibility, and the restrained encounter between the sexes). Traditional gender identities and roles thus underlie Islamic authoritarianism.

Overpoliticization of the Islamic utopia—a yearning for the holistic implementation of the three pillars of Islam, the three D's of *"din, dünya ve devlet,"* (faith-religion, life-world, and state)[46]—leads to totalizing conceptions of identity, religion, and state. This utopian dimension is one of the distinctive traits of Islamist movements and distinguishes them from other "new social movements." Only self-limitation of Islamism as a political project and the autonomization of Islam within civil society will open up Islam as a space for diversity and pluralism. However, gender questions will remain the yardstick by which Islamic pluralism is measured.

Thus, the direction in which Islamist movements evolve will hinge significantly on the elaboration and recognition of women's identity and agency. Paradoxically, Islamic politics can delimit women's individuality and visibility at the same time that the politicization of women within Islamic politics empowers Muslim women. Muslim women are empowered by an Islamism that assigns them a "militant," "missionary," political identity, and by secular education, which provides them a "professional," "intellectual" legitimacy. The new public visibility of Muslim women, who are outspoken, militant, and educated, brings about a shift in the semiotics of veiling, which has long evoked the traditional, subservient domestic roles of Muslim women. The new veiling represents the public and collective affirmation of women who are searching for recognition of their Muslim identity through its expression—that is, through Islamism. Islamism, as the "politics of recognition,"[47] empowers Muslim women, providing intellectual and political tools for asserting their long-silenced difference, by questioning the equation between *civilized* and *Westernized*. It also empowers them by supplying a collective identity. Furthermore, Islamic politics provides a realm of opportunities for their "self-realization" and becomes a vehicle for their public and professional visibility. Women now work as columnists and journalists; they attend political meetings, militate for the Islamist party, write best-selling novels, and make films—all inspired by the new language of Islamism. An elite cadre of Islamic women is thus emerging from within Islamism.

Woman's participation in Islamism has had unintended consequences; a latent individuation of women is at work. Women, once empowered by their public and professional visibility, continue to follow and develop personal life strategies. At the same time, while never forgetting the primacy of their identities as mothers and wives, women confront and criticize the Islamist ideology. The exit from the *mahrem* (domestic intimate) sphere forces women to question traditional gender identities and male definitions of "licit" and "illicit" behavior, thereby unveiling relations of power between Islamist men and women. Criticizing the "pseudoprotectionism" of Muslim men, veiled women claim their right to "acquire personality"—that is, "a life of their own"—and, consequently, provoke disorder in Islamic gender definitions and identities.

Hence, the title *Forbidden Modern* conveys a double meaning. First, *forbidden* refers to the gendered construct of the private sphere (*mahrem*). The moral psychology of the domestic sphere depends on woman's controlled sexuality, which is guaranteed by woman's corporal and behavioral modesty (exemplified by veiling) as well as by limiting encounters between the sexes (social segregation of the sexes). Veiling suggests modesty, the forbidden woman. Yet, through Islamism and modernism, women have acquired public forms of visibility, sharing with men the same urban, political, and educational territories. Again under the veil, a new profile of Muslim woman is emerging, which in turn constitutes a threat to the moral psychology of gender identifications. Second, *Forbidden Modern* points to this encounter of women with modernity which is taking place in practice but is "forbidden" in principle by Islamism. It is these paradoxes, ambiguities, and unfolding tensions—between the politicization of Islam and the individuation of woman, between the Islamist utopia and personal strategies for women, between the quest for authenticity and that for native modernity—that I present in this book.

Postpublication: Engaging Nonengagement

The readings and reactions to a book, which provide a context for inquiry and discussion, can say more about a subject than the book itself. And the nonpolitical engagement opens up a new space for understanding and dialogue, which itself can become more engaging to the extent that is identified by the author.

In the preface to the Turkish edition of this book, I wrote about my deliberate intention to not locate myself in the political debate and polarization, by then very fierce, between Islamists and secularists on the "headscarf issue." I also explained that I refused to adopt secularist, feminist, Islamist, or leftist perspectives to explain the Islamist veiling movement (thereby facing a significant loss of readership). I tried to define my location as a sociologist by maintaining "analytic distance"—that is, distance not justified by an objective analysis using scientific-positivist arguments but, rather, by sociological analysis, itself derived from its relationship with human action. I distanced myself from the compelling political arguments by naming my limited enterprise as an aesthetic interpretation; as a sociologist, I wanted to understand the actors' point of view by employing sociological empathy (without being swayed by ideology, neither by sympathy nor aversion), and not as an ethical assertion of general principles (here again I would lose credibility by doing so). The metaphor I used was that in my project I was an artisan: as the carver works with the diamond to increase its brilliance, the researcher works with a multifaceted social reality to shed light on it.

I do not know if Islamist veiling gained more clarity and intelligibility because of my work, but it is certain that, according to the radical secularists, because I studied it without denouncing it, I was responsible for Islamism's increasing political force and intellectual legitimacy in Turkey. On the other hand, for the radical Islamists I was not telling their story exactly, not taking into account their "becoming" in the future, but making a synchronistic analysis of their encounter with modernity, which, they believe, is anachronistic to their Islamic utopia.

Rejecting the master-narratives of modernization, secularization, and the emancipation of woman, society, and the state as the most cherished and history-making public narrative of Turkey—known simply as Kemalism—on the one hand, and not affiliating myself with the counter-narratives of Islamism, leftism, or neofeminism, on the other, I was simply dislocated. The category of "intellectual" defined in the Turkish experience by master narratives, requires political engagement either in terms of critical or supportive proximity to the state. Hence, my calling for "nonengagement" with the subject of my study accounts for the loss of the intellectual credibility I was disempowered since such credibility is defined through collective identity and the use of master-narratives (fostering the postmodern trivialization of myself).

The shifting role of the intellectual from one who interprets universal and rational laws of change to one who studies emotion and interest-laden agency, examining ambiguous, paradoxical, multifaceted, polymorphous indigeneous practices in an effort to introduce actor, subjectivity, and non-Western particularisms is not easily acknowledged in the highly politicized Turkish context. It is neither considered nor criticized as simple postmodern playfulness and relativism. Although in some of the reviews of my book I received the postmodern label, in general I was treated more "seriously." In some contexts giving voice to particularisms and studying agency, especially with regard to Islamism, is almost synonymous with being "reactionary" and "fundamentalist."[48] Thus, if one crosses over intellectual and class boundaries, especially by working from within such central issues as Islam and women, the appearance of intellectual engagement becomes almost a matter of "impurity."

The readings of *Modern Mahrem* rendered by Turkish intellectuals and different segments of society provide feedback for further understanding of Islamist veiling and the power relations in which it is contextualized. Overall Turkish readers (unlike many French ones),[49] were not very receptive to ambiguities within the text, and consequently, they have denied almost all double meanings, borrowings, and hybridizations. Both for the Islamists and the modernists it was either Islam or modernity, either Islamic women or feminist women.[50] I myself, as a by-product of these mutually exclusive realities, and particularly that of Westernism and secularism, was "misperceived" by both Islamists and Kemalists. During a television interview (on a program similar to "Cross-Fire"), the Islamists were unwilling to match my physical appearance (uncovered and not very modest for Islamist taste) with what I was saying, while the Kemalists felt betrayed because they had expected to hear a courageous political denouncement of Islamism. Audiences sympathetic to both sides of the debate expressed their anger and criticism in anonymous letters to me.

At first this book, and its author, were caught in the polarization between Islamists and secularists. Talk of "hidden agendas" and "conspiracy theories" obscured and hijacked other approaches, analyses, and interviews. Gradually, however, the position of obstinate nonengagement in the ongoing polemics, within the proscribed terms, opened up a novel space for dialogue and interaction.

The dialogue and recognition between different social actors is possible only when the walls of incommunicability are deconstructed and demystified when the "other" is "desatanized." As the Turkish edition of *The Forbidden Modern* contributed to lessening the distances between representations, it contributed also to the displacement of the terms of the debate and the establishment of relations of exchange and reciprocity between Islamists, secularists, and feminists.

Two anecdotes regarding encounters with two divergent types of women are very telling. One concerns the personal comments of a very distinguished novelist, Adalet Ağaoğlu, and the other those of an anonymous group of veiled students. Adalet Ağaoğlu told me that she stopped reading the book after the third chapter, which depicted Kemalist women who participated in the public space at the expense of their individuality and sexuality. To emphasize this intrinsic tension, the chapter ended with references to her novel *Lie Down for Death*, in which the publicly "emancipated" heroine commits suicide upon discovering her own sexual desires. Ağaoğlu criticized me for using her own novel to suggest that women like her no longer had anything to say. Her comments forced me to become aware of a central question I had dismissed but which the book itself could not avoid. The suicide of a Kemalist women at the end of one chapter and the sudden eruption of the veiled women in the following one—along with the gap, the discontinuity, and the silence between the two chapters—all hinted at a reversal of a situation, at least in the sense of a paradigmatic shift in self-definition.

The veiled Muslim students were indeed intensely preoccupied by their new self-definitions. On their invitation I participated in a panel on "Modernization, Women, and Islam" organized by the Faculty of Theology at the University of Marmara, which three hundred students attended. Half of the audience consisted of women dressed in Islamic outfits, who sat together in the front seats of the conference room. I sat with the male panelists but exchanged gazes with the female students, wondering if there really was a common langugage beneath our radically distinct corporal statements. I wondered if I had something to say that would be received sympathetically, or if I was totally misdirected and misproved by my research. Male Islamist commentators (also professors) were, in general, arguing that Islam was recognizing full equality of rights for men and women. In response, female students asked me if males can truly defend women's rights and if they can speak on women's behalf as well as women can themselves. Quoting the book, they addressed me with a host of questions, ranging from "How does one combine domesticity with individual professional aspirations?" to "How do we preserve the difference of feminity in the public male domain?" Their questions made me think that they were far ahead of the book in elaborating their identities. Furthermore, they were using not only the book but also its author in their struggles with conservative male counterparts for their self-affirmation. After the panel a group of female students came up to me and presented themselves playfully as "modern *mahrem*" and let me know that they had had a long debate with male students in their faculty club on the issue of the segregation of the sexes. These students had found a way to assert themselves and succeeded in organizing a panel for "all." I was used as a tool for them to transgress boundaries. Nonengagement had unintentionally become more engaging.

CHAPTER 2

Woman: The Touchstone of Westernization

In 1910, at a time when the Ottoman Empire was undergoing profound changes, Ottoman princess Seniha Sultan, exasperated by the manner in which the West represented the conditions under which Turkish women were assumed to live, wrote a letter to her French friend Madame Simone de la Cherté:

> My dear! We, Turkish women, are not known in Europe at all. I can even say that we are much less known than Chinese and Japanese women. Regardless of how far Peking and Tokyo are from Paris . . . Istanbul is nearby, though.
>
> They make up really unimaginable stories about us. Not important! They anticipate us to be slaves, to be imprisoned in rooms, to live only behind lattice windows, to be chained up and watched over by ferocious black and other slaves who are armed from head to foot and who are also thought to put us into sacks and then throw us into the Bosphorus from time to time. We are assumed to live in a group of numerous rivaling wives, and they expect every Turkish man to have a harem of his own, that is, to have at least eight or ten wives.[1]

This letter exemplifies how the Western world, both in the writings of travelers of the period and in the works of Orientalists, concerned itself with the disturbing yet simultaneously exotic difference of Eastern societies. Edward Said, in *Orientalism*, illustrates how the West creates its culture and identity by differentiating itself from the "East," relegating the latter to an "inferior" and "repressed" other. He asserts that Western culture reproduces the very ideas and images related to the Orient in imagery as well as in scientific and political discourses.[2] For Said the Western representation of the Orient, deemed the surrogate to even the darker side of the Occident, indeed helps the West to gain its strength and identity.[3]

The narration on Ottoman women by the Princess of Belgiojoso, who was in exile in Turkey in 1853, offers an example of Western "astonishment" in regard to so-called Eastern primitiveness: "The women do not have any sense of shame either for their children or for people around them; they can easily undress in front of their sons; they can freely talk about intimate issues in their presence."[4] The display of Ottoman women's femininity and sexuality within the closed space of the harem in a "natural" fashion is critically depicted from the standpoint of the "puritan" morality of the era. The princess proposed a modernization for the Ottoman state that requires essentially the abolition of Islam, which is considered to be what separates the East from the "civilized" world. As she maintained, the very constitution of a new family form similar to the Western model, in contrast to existing polygamous marriages, would be the most substantial reform of all in this modernization attempt.

These convictions indeed spring from the Western ideology of humanism, and they were exercised exclusively during the modernization attempts initiated by the Ottoman ruling elites during the nineteenth century. So long as the West determined the very definition of modernity and formed its propulsive force on a global scale, on the strength of ideas originating from the Enlightenment tradition and the industrial civilization it created, societies of the Orient lost their decision-making power, and were successively forced to define their culture and history in reference to the Western model. Those societies that were "weak" in terms of generating social change and innovation as an indigenous structural process were, thus, dependent on the impact of Western modernity and its local constructs. Here the concept of "weak historicity" is useful in highlighting this dependence in sociological terms rather than reducing it to economic parameters. It gives priority to the analysis of social representation and agency in non-Western societies, which are not, of course, independent of the problematic representations of Western modernity. [5]

It is the societies that lagged behind in the process of social innovation, or, more accurately, the making of the principles of modernity, that sought their histories constantly in reference to the precepts of Western modernity. Hence, as Iranian philosopher Daryush Shayegan argues, those societies left on the periphery of Western civilization are excluded from the sphere of history and knowledge, for they cannot participate any longer in the "carnival of change," and this exclusion has in turn resulted in a sense of "cultural schizophrenia" in these cultures. [6]

Thus, the encounter of the East with the Western world resulted in at least the disintegration of the Eastern identity, rather than in a reciprocal exchange between the two cultures. Hichem Djait, a Tunisian, expresses his opinion of the rise of the West and the decline of Islam as follows: "The history of Islam does not act on the basis of its own dynamics; it rather seems to be a reversed and wilted reflection of the West."[7]

If we examine the history of Turkey, it is possible to detect a voluntary commitment especially by the Kemalists in the service of establishing a cultural liaison with the West. [8] The Turkish case of modernization is an excellent example in terms of the course of action taken in the adoption of the Western rationalist and universalist model and the principle of secularism itself. As much as anything else, these modernization attempts gave rise to a discussion of the question of the East-West opposition in a society in which Islamic culture is deeply embedded. The history of ideas in Turkey reflects the opposition between the Islamic and Westernist viewpoints and their two distinct projects for society. Much more than anything else, outlooks regarding the social position of women lie at the center of these debates. For it is indeed the attitudes about the position women should occupy in society that set the course of action a society can take and that mark the limits of modernization in Muslim societies. This is why in these societies "the question of women" is not defined only in relation to the social conditions in which women live but is also related to the issues of culture and civilization. Although the most visible feature of the Turkish modernization movement is its transition from a patrimonial Islamic empire to a secular national state, the increasing public visibility of women in social life and the principle of equality between men and women has helped introduce the ideals of modernity into the collective imagination of a Muslim country. In contrast to the political transformation which targeted the state apparatus, the cultural renewals at the interpersonal level and between the sexes in fact have followed a slow, less striking, yet as I will demonstrate, concurrently more weighty course of action.

The condition of women in Turkey has evolved along with the historical course of modernization attempts. The question of women lies at the center of the modernization mentality, which favored the Western notion of universality in opposition to tradition, and particularly, Islam. While the Westernized elites defended the idea that Western universalism could only be achieved if women were emancipated from Islamic traditions, the conservatives were suspicious, if not hostile, to attempts at "liberating" women from their traditional roles.

At the expense of oversimplification, it is possible to evaluate the history of modernization in Turkey as the history of two conflicting cultural models or two movements—the Westernist and the Islamist. The contents of these two movements were naturally subject to modifications as they faced changing social issues through time; consequently, the reformism of the Tanzimat Period (reforms initiated between 1839 and 1876 to westernize the political, social, and economic structures of the Ottoman Empire) does not equal the Westernism of the republican era. The Westernist movements searched for the key to progress in Western universalism, whereas, for the traditionalist and later Islamist movements, only the revival of Islam and its application to everyday life and state governance could assure salvation.[9]

The position of women is the determining factor in these conflicts framing the existing dualities, such as Islam/the West, traditional/modern, equality/difference, and *mahrem*/*namahrem* (private/public). While for the Westernists equality between the sexes and the participation of liberated women in the public realm is a prerequisite of "social development," for the Islamists, the exit of women from private life, *mahrem*, is an attempt to undermine existing communitarian rules, which may result in the moral decay of society. In other words, the affinity between these two movements originates in their views with regard to the position of women in society.[10] Hence, discussions of the appropriate position for women in Muslim countries directly refer to preferences for different social models.

Women and the Consciousness of Civilization

The social position of women began to be discussed with the onset of modernization attempts during the Tanzimat Period (1839–1876), along with the orientation toward the Western social model. During this period the duality between the West and the East was formulated upon the differentiation of the material and spiritual definitions of civilization. For intellectuals of this period the fundamental question was to determine for which features of the reforms Islam would provide support and with which features it would conflict and, thus, to agree upon mutually shared reforms with Islam. The ultimate question that needed to be answered was whether any convergence existed between West and East. This duality existed in every course of thought oriented toward Ottoman society during the period. As a consequence, the social position of women was discussed within the boundaries of this framework from the time of the Tanzimat reforms to the Second Constitution (1908–1919). Those who emphasized the universality of Western civilization in their arguments criticized arranged marriages, polygamous marriages, and discrimination between the sexes; they defended the right of education for women and accepted romantic love as a basis for marriage. Those, however, who perceived the consequences of these Western-oriented reforms as a threat to the dominant cultural model stressed the importance of preserving the traditional position of women in society.

Thus, based on the impacts of the West upon the modernization of Ottoman society, two cultural and social propositions emerged. The first proposition sought to establish the future along with the support of the past; it argued that the cultural and moral inheritance of the past ought to be preserved, and, as a consequence, the impacts of Western civilization needed to be confined to technological, administrative, and material aspects. The second proposition, however, argued that the civilization maintained a totality in itself. Adherents to this proposition basically aim to transform or reinterpret traditions in the attempt to achieve modernity. Thus, for the reformists the education and liberation of women was a prerequisite of civilization, while for the traditionalists the framing of relationships between men and women according to the Sharia was necessary to preserve the spiritual values and morality of society. The disputes of this period demonstrate that the issue of women's role in society lay at the very center of these two conflicting viewpoints. [11]

Mahmud Esad (1856–1918), one of the representatives of the traditionalist paradigm, criticized reformist intellectuals who attributed the reasons for backwardness to the Sharia and existing polygamous marriages. Disputing the reformists, he maintained that this tradition in fact originated from the very nature of human beings—that is, that polygamy is a natural law—and it is the Sharia that legitimates this tradition.[12] Defending polygamy as a practice compatible with nature, and even as a beneficial rule of society in terms of the elimination of prostitution, Esad asserted that the superiority of Islamic civilization over Christian was to be sought in the spiritual world and moral codes.[13]

Esad referred to the binary opposition of the spiritual and material components of civilization when he wrote: "there exist two sides of every civilization, one of them is material and the other one is the spiritual side. The spiritual side refers to the morality of this civilization. The material side, however, consists of sewing machines, railways and dreadnoughts, in short, it is the visible products of industrial inventions."[14] According to this distinction, the spiritual side of civilization is composed of moral acquisitions, while the material side refers to industrial inventions and the production of goods. As maintained by this argument, it is possible to adopt the material side of Western civilization so long as the moral civilization of the East is preserved in the society. The conservative outlook, which differentiated the material and spiritual aspects of civilization in such a manner, was ready to transfer the technology of the West, provided that the "belief system, morality and spirit" of the society would be provided by Eastern civilization.[15]

The Westernists, who defended the idea that Western civilization is a totality and cannot be separated into distinct parts, argued that modernization could only be built upon universal values, not cultural particularisms. This outlook approached civilization as a monolithic entity and rejected the distinction between cultural and scientific knowledge. Hence, one of the representatives of this tradition, Şemseddin Sami (1850–1914), argued that, "in case the West was inferior in the cultural realm, it would not be able to develop its material civilization."[16]

As for his Westernist and republican intellectual successors, Sami, too, treated the education and rights of women within the framework of the "civilization project." Sami, who wrote that "the condition of any society is always symmetrical to the condition of women," defended the idea that "the whole of humanity will be educated, once women are given the right of education."[17] For him society would not be able to develop and attain civilization so long as half of the population (i.e., women) in the Ottoman society remained ignorant, idle, and uneducated. If they were educated in science and taught morality, they could transmit this knowledge to their children. Thus, the right to education for women was defended both as a way to glorify their motherhood tasks and in the name of civilization.

In contrast to the naturalist arguments of the conservatives, Sami defined the position of women with reference to their social conditions and particularly in terms of their right to education. In his book *Kadınlar (Women)* he defended the idea that both women and men have similar intellectual faculties. Further, he maintained that societies will always minimize the possible services women can provide unless they acknowledge the intelligence of women. He even cited some of the possible occupations at which women would be better than men "thanks to their natural inclinations": tailors, medical workers, service workers, and accountants in trade.[18]

As a representative of the reformist outlook of the Tanzimat Period, Sami defended Islam, claiming that it did not act as a barrier to progress and civilization; indeed, it was the misinterpretations of Islam that give rise to certain problems. He stated that the hotly debated issues of the period such as polygamy, veiling, the exit of women from *mahrem*, and divorce were not directly affiliated with Islam, and that these issues arose from a lack of knowledge concerning the "real orders and laws" of Islam. He claimed that the ban on the exit of women from *mahrem* and their slavery were all practiced prior to Islam, and that the religion of Islam itself opposes such social traditions. In relation to the practice of slavery he further maintains that Islam does not order slavery at all and that the liberation of a slave is regarded as one of the most important examples of a pious act; yet Islam did not abolish the institution of slavery. Sami emphasized the fact that the practice of veiling did not bar women, who are mentioned in the Koran, from taking part in meetings and other activities, voting, and even going to war. As far as the question of polygamy was considered, he backed the argument that the practice of polygamy was not invented by Islam and that, although Islam stated that "it is pious to suffice oneself with one wife," this statement was not used in practice.[19]

The different interpretations of Islam in relation to the position of women by the traditionalists and the Westernists became evident in the controversy that took place between traditionalist Esad and the famous female writer of the period, Fatma Aliye (1864–1924).[20] Referring to the verse of the Koran that legitimized monogamous marriages, Aliye, the first "intellectual" woman to emerge from private education at home, attempted to falsify the arguments of Esad defending polygamy as a "natural law," confirmed by Şeriat, the religious law.[21] As Aliye explained, in fact the rules set up initially by Islam have degenerated over time; Islam in fact does not oppose the rights of woman, and it does not serve as a barrier to the "progress of civilization." This controversy was first published in a periodical ("Malumat" 1896), and later Fatma Aliye developed her ideas in a book on Muslim women (in 1900) that was also translated into Arabic and French.

The position of women in society and women's social functions were discussed during the Tanzimat Period with regard to the determination of how far attempts at Westernization would go. Authors of this period, including Namık Kemal (1840–1888) and Ahmet Mithad Efendi (1844–1912), used paired concepts such as *Şark-Garp* (East-West) and *Alafrangalık-Alaturkalık* (occidental style–oriental style) in discussing distinctions between the West and the East. These authors stressed the significance of the empire's constant orientation toward the West and the need to differentiate the good and the bad attributes of civilization (material and spiritual aspects) that Islam does not hinder progress. For instance, Namık Kemal, an author who symbolizes this period in his writings, "is neither a Sharia supporter nor an Easternist nor a Westernist without any reservation," and he was also aware of the dangers of "conservatism of the old" and "imitations of the new."[22]

The myth of the Golden Age of Islam, referring to the idea that the new rights that will be granted to women as a consequence of modernization attempts will not conflict with the practices of early Islam and that every novelty to be adapted from the West can be detected within the sources of Islam, exercised a profound influence upon the Westernists of the period.[23] The Westernist movement thus pursued the sources of legitimacy within Islam. Ahmet Mithad Efendi and Namık Kemal indeed referred to the religion of Islam as the zenith of civilization, with its emphasis on moral values and on the training of honorable individuals.[24]

Jale Parla has suggested Tanzimat did not generate a "dualistic culture" between Eastern and Western norms in Ottoman cultural life, but it did provide a platform for discussion on the "orientation towards the West of which boundaries were definitive and confined" and which was "reinforced with various verses and *hadiths*" (the tradition of the Prophet Muhammed—i.e., his sayings) "under the umbrella of a dominant Islamic culture."[25] Parla also notices a latent and ardent desire for a "father figure" among writers of the Tanzimat Period.[26] According to Parla, Tanzimat intellectuals aspired to resurrect a sultan, a father figure who would preserve the morality of the East at the societal as well as the familial level.[27] The most serious threat to the authority of the father, however, did not spring from the science and technology of the West but, rather, from "physical lust." As a consequence of the detachment from Islam, Tanzimat intellectuals worried that lust would replace "spiritual love" and would seduce all youngsters, resulting in their "running after evil women."[28] Departing from the rules of Islamic training and aspiring for the West are all rendered equal to the arousal of sensual and sexual desires. Along these lines, Namık Kemal wrote that "there exists no difference between dancing and flirting with the devil"; and "if what you assume to be civilization is seeing women in the streets almost naked or dancing at a gathering, these are all against our morality. We do not want it, we *do not* !"[29]

The importance assigned to the privacy (*mahremiyet*) of women during the Tanzimat Period can be seen in the laws confining women to invisibility not only socially but physically as well. For instance, the population census recorded the physical attributes of men—age, height, eye color, beard, etc.—while women are only registered by name and age, and, interestingly enough, only by their relatives.[30] The civil code, too, served to protect women's privacy. The units of a house that are designated as women's quarters (*makarr-i nisvan*)—such as the kitchen, well, and courtyard—were by law not to be visible from neighboring houses. A neighbor who can see any part of the women's quarters was obliged to block the view of these quarters with a partition.[31]

It is clear that ever since the Tanzimat Period the boundaries of Westernization have been determined with regard to the issues of the privacy of women and the relationship between the two sexes. To put it differently, Westernization and the arousal of "civilizational" consciousness were directly dependent upon the relationship between the sexes, the allocation of space, and lifestyles. The boundaries between *mahrem* and *namahrem*, the interior and exterior of a house, and the regulations dictated in relation to these realms, as well as the lives of women, were affected as a consequence of changes following the Tanzimat Period. Fashion magazines, free of the censorship exercised by Abdülhamid II (1876–1909), provided space for articles on hair and skin care as well as the use of cosmetics in their pages; veiled women registered for Swedish physical exercise courses, and female students of the School of Fine Arts used Greek statues, covered with waist cloths, as their models.[32] The increasing education of women, their emergence from their houses into the public realm, their interest in exercise and dancing, and all other activities undertaken by women after the Tanzimat Period symbolized not only the Western lifestyle but, more important, the increasing socialization and visibility of women.

The main reason why Westernists and conservatives focused their debates on the issues related to women is bound up with the degeneration of *mahrem* (privacy) itself. The female body, which long established the boundaries between the realms of *mahrem* and *namahrem*, still influences social projects. Therefore, it is not mere coincidence that the Islamist movement that emerged in the 1980s in Turkey has chosen these two symbolic realms in narrating its ideological struggle.

It was during the Tanzimat Period that the most salient difference between the West and the East was delineated, in terms of interior/exterior, *mahrem/namahrem*, and thus relations between men and women. It was also during this period that the very essence of Westernization was conceived for the first time as "the project of civilization," which meant the transformation of Muslim traditional social organization and ways of life.

Western Equality, Islamic Morality, and Turkish Tradition

The period of the Constitutional Monarchy, 1908–1919 (called the Second Constitution because of the short-lived efforts to institute a constitution in 1876–1878), was the time during which various intellectual outlooks flourished and the issues of citizenship and the equality of women in Ottoman society dominated the public agenda, regardless of the deterioration of the empire. For T. Taşkiran (1903–1979), this was a period of "Great Hopes," while for Ziya Gökalp (1876–1924) it was the "New Life." Furthermore, the intellectual outlooks that originated and crystallized during this period underlay the succeeding Kemalist reforms.

The three intellectual outlooks of the period, Islamic, Westernist, and Turkist, all defined their ideological bases in support of the "restoration" of the empire, while they diverged from one another in their approaches to the rights of women.[33] In fact, all of the reformist movements of this period were supporters of the idea of "progress" and were oriented toward the Western model. The fundamental problem was to determine how far the Westernization movement would be tolerated by the Islamic culture. Hence, Ismail Kara suggests that it would be much more reasonable to regard the Islamic movement of the Constitutional Period not as an opposition to Westernization but, rather, as the Islamization of these attempts.[34] The converging point of the Islamic, Western-oriented, and Turkist movements of the period was their emphasis on the idea of progress and the fact that they were all Westernist reformist attempts in their basic orientations. However, they maintained different approaches to the question of identity. The definitive yet distinct reference points of identity and civilization distinguish these outlooks—the Western universal, the Islamic, and the ancient Turkish values. It is therefore more productive to focus on the issue of civilization identity rather than of Westernization, which also leads us directly to the question of women. For the relationship between women and men as well as the organization and regulation of interior versus exterior provide a basis for cultural identity.

Thus, the question of women remained powerful in determining the limits of modernism (i.e., the orientation toward the Western cultural model) set by the ideological movements of this period. Issues of *mahrem* (private) life and the relationship between the sexes were among the most resistant of established cultural elements to the Western cultural model, due to the fact that they were regulated by religious law. Westernists deemed the traditions of Islam a barrier against civilization, and they sought the liberation of women from the chains of these traditions, whereas the Islamists accused the Westernists of being imitators and favored the preservation of the moral values of a Muslim society and loyalty to Sharia. The Turkists, however, sought the elements of an ideal society of the future in past Turkish life, and they did not confine moral identity to the religion of Islam.

Women as Human Beings

The radical Westernist movement of this period tried to define civilization independently from religion and tradition. According to the arguments of Westernism, which were formulated on the premises of rationalism and positivism, civilization is a product of neither Islam nor Christianity, but, rather, is the product of contemporary and universal humanist values. For thinkers with this outlook attempts to differentiate the good and bad aspects of civilization were nothing more than implicit anti-Westernism.[35] As stated by Abdullah Cevdet (186?–1932), one of the founders of *Ittihat ve Terakki Cemiyeti* (Union of Order and Progress), Western civilization is "a totality which must be accepted with its roses and thorns."[36] For the radical Westernists, Islamic traditions served as the most salient barrier in the path toward civilization. This is why Cevdet cited religious rules regarding veiling and polygamy, together with "degenerated traditions," as the main reasons for the backwardness of Muslims as well as for the breakdown of the empire. [37]

The most radical criticism of traditionalist and religious morality appeared in the poems of Tevfik Fikret (1867–1915). Fikret, who wanted to replace religious morality with "*humanisme*," felt that it is reason that seeks truth and argues for "justice" in opposition to "the tyrannical God" who enslaves human beings. He stressed his profound belief in the transformative power of reason.[38] The Western radicalism of Tevfik Fikret lay in his attempts to detach the sources of morality from tradition and religion.[39] For Fikret the rights of women should be defined within the framework of human rights. The following verse from a Fikret poem represents a common view about the question of women in the Constitutional Period:

Humiliation is not a woman's lot in life, of course,
All humanity will be abased should all women be miserable.[40]

Salahaddin Asım explicity depicted the treatment of women as "female beings" rather than as "human beings" in religious tradition and their consequent segregation from civilization in his book *Türk Kadınlığının Tereddisi yahud Karılaşmak (The Degeneration of Turkish Women, or Womanization).*[41] Asim severely criticized the fact that Turkish women only undertook their motherhood and wifely tasks in response to religious laws and were otherwise detached from social functions. Defining this condition, which solely serves "lust and reproduction," as "womanization," he called for the liberation of women from the status of female beings in order to become human beings. Regarding this issue in terms of "the question of civilization and of women," Asim diagnosed religion as the main cause of "Turkish womanization," which was, as he saw it, the expression of a social illness. He believed that it was the practice of veiling that lay behind the backwardness of Ottoman Turks in terms of "society and civilization." Furthermore, for him the nature of the relationship between men and women and the determinant moral values were all dependent upon veiling. Thus "veiling" represented the "initial and the most decisive characteristic which differentiates society from Western and Christian manners." In the chapter of his book devoted to the question of veiling he called for a sociological analysis of this issue. Meanwhile, he argued that, where "material veiling" is practiced, it is society that treats women merely as female beings and in which the only social service assigned to them is related to "lust," yet in contemporary societies women are no longer veiled and their independent identities are recognized. He agrees with the statement that veiling, the "reason as well as the outcome of the treatment of women as female beings, separates women from civilized life."[42]

In his unusual yet severe criticism of the glorification of the motherhood and wifehood roles of Turkish and Muslim women, Asim further stated that a woman would never be a "civilized human being" and would not "qualify as an independent social person" when she remained, on the one hand, "the slave and mate of her husband" and, on the other, "the servant and feeder of her children like cows."[43] Giving credit to the argument that women would be recognized as civilized human beings if and only if they participated in social life, he brought a feminist theme into the discussion with his reference to the affinity between the questions of social liberation and the socialization of women (the acquisition of social functions by women). Salahaddin Asim was among the first of those who spoke of women as individuals. In conjunction with the relationship he saw between veiling and male domination, he claimed that veiling "eradicates the individuality" and "remains indifferent to the personal honor" of women and, further, that women were "excluded from society and civilization in the name of and on account of men." Stating his argument as follows, "the honor of women is convicted and imprisoned due to the fact that the public conscience has not yet recognized their independent individuality," he suggested that veiling "originates from the greed and lust" of men. Finally, he expressed his opinion that the practice of veiling will be abolished with the greater individualization and increasing liberation of women from men.[44]

The Westernist outlook of the Constitutional Period drew parallels between the rights of women and social progress. Hence, another Westernist author, Celal Nuri Ileri (1881–1938), in his book *Kadınlarımız (Our Women)*, drew attention to the rights of women as the initiators of the "advancement of Turks," arguing that:

> The operation should not start with the army and the navy. It is not even reasonable to initiate progress in the schools. We had better start with the improvement of the conditions women live in so that, in turn, they will do the same for their children, and thus, their children, once they grow up, will reconcile the State and the people. The construction of a building does not start from its roof. It starts from the base. The woman is the base of the human building.[45]

This passage demonstrates the extent to which the themes of social progress, civilized life, and the education and liberation of women from Islamic tradition began to dominate discussions during this period preceding the modern Turkish Republic. For Westernist thinkers the liberation of women corresponded to their attainment of the status of human being. What is interesting is that, by this reasoning, women would not reach the status of human being for their own sakes but would be serving society in its attempt to rise to the level of "civilized." According to this outlook, equality between the sexes emerges as a necessary condition in the formation of modern families and the actualization of this goal requires the training of both sons and daughters in this direction.

Halit Hamit, the author of *Kadınlık Aleminde Tam Eşitlik (Complete Equality in the World of Women)*, maintained that "you must train and raise children who will hold ideas in favor of women. Your son should hate misogynists. Your daughter must recognize her rights and must have the self-power to attain them."[46] He was the first person in Turkey to defend the political rights of women as natural rights and as a social necessity, claiming that "being a deputy is a need of women as well." For him "the age of humanity" would commence only when women, too, take their place in political and administrative affairs (e.g., in parliament), since humanism, above all, means equal rights for everybody.

Under the guidance of the principles of humanism it was held that Ottoman society would enter into the era of civilization following women's advancement to the level of humanity, thanks to the ideal of equality. Contrary to the Tanzimat Period, modernists of the Constitutional Period defined the essence of civilization with reference to the cultural structure rather than to the technological gains of society. In other words, positivisim and humanism, both of which assisted Western civilization in attaining the status of a universal reference point, fed the works of Westernist thinkers.

According to these thinkers, rationalist Western civilization, defined independently of Christianity, was applicable everywhere at any time. The principles of liberation and rationality, which indeed addressed the whole of mankind, opened up a path to civilization. Islamic traditions, on the other hand, were assumed to obstruct the way to Westernstyle civilization and social progress. In this frame of mind the liberation of women was equated with the accomplishment of civilization. The abandonment of veiling as the symbol of Islamic traditions would mean the emancipation of women and their attainment of the status of human beings. Thus, the emergence of women from privacy to participation in (civilized) social life by means of education lies at the very center of the Westernization project. Given the importance assigned to education and the participation of women in social life during the early republican era (and even the idea that men should endorse the emancipation of women), it is clear that the connection between the rights of women and the project of civilization was indeed established by the Westernist course of thought.

Veiling against Lust

Contrary to the propositions of Westernists, in which the idea of social progress becomes associated with the advancement of women to the "level of humanity," Islamism draws attention to the moral purity of women and to the danger of breakdown in the "community" as a consequence of weakened loyalty to religious rules.

According to Islamic thought during the Constitutional Period, the maintenance of the empire was entirely dependent upon the widespread and decisive exercise of Sharia laws in society. Furthermore, this outlook maintained that the exchange with modern civilization would take place only after the fundamental realities of Islamic morality had been actualized, and, above all, this exchange should have been confined to the scientific and technological spheres.

Islamists, who were distressed by the negative effects of the 1908 reforms on women, utterly opposed attempts to liberate women. Writing in French, Said Halim Pasha (1863–1921) criticized Westernists and argued that there could only be a negative relationship between civilization and the liberation of women: "None of the civilizations in the world starts with the liberation of women; on the contrary, it is an undisputable fact of history that all civilizations in which women attained complete freedom declined." [47]

For Said Halim the abandonment of veiling, women's companionship with men, and their beginning to live like "Western" women constituted "social dangers." Distinguishing between political and social (communitarian) liberation, he argued that the essence of what Turkish women require is "social rather than political." Said Halim claimed that the supporters of women's liberation have aimed particularly at "the abolition of the harem and the establishment of relationships and communication between women and men as is prevalent in Western societies," and he further stated that the liberation of women would lead to a "pleasure-oriented," hedonistic society rather than a "society of decency and virtue."[48] He even proposed the establishment of an association for the "protection of society," which socially responsible men and women would join.[49]

The duality between the "virtues of Islam" and "prodigal Western civilization" depicts the significance of morality in the Islamic outlook. For Islamists, who were against "*meyhane*, whorehouses, dancing, bars, theater and all other such prodigal institutions,"[50] Islam itself would obscure the development of such a prodigal civilization. For them, it is only the morality of Islam, in the service of protecting social laws, that would be able to resist Western civilization which acts as the agent of liberation and permissiveness.

Musa Kazım (1858–1920) (the highest official religious authority for several years in the early 1900s) even called on the state to act so as to ensure loyalty to religious laws and the exercise of penalties for those who were disobedient. In his discussion of the idea of liberty, which originated during the Constitutional Period, he argued that for human beings to live together in a society (i.e., social life) freedom should be regulated not only by secular laws but by religious rules as well, and he placed the veiling of women at the top of these rules. He expressed his distress over the abandonment of veiling, which is assumed to ensure morality and order in society. With regard to the abandonment of veiling he stated that: "Upon the declaration of our new Constitution, unfortunately, it became possible to witness that some [women] do not obey this rule anymore and, God forbid, it is even heard that a mischievous situation is about to emerge among Muslims."[51]

Regarding the veiling of women as an essential part of Sharia, Kazim deemed veiling a protection against the "lust between men and women" and a prerequisite to family happiness. Muslim women "should be dressed in a manner inconducive to lust and must not show themselves to the lustful gazes of foreigners." As he maintained, "the only reason why woman was created is to enable the procreation and training of children."[52] Thus, to him the engagement of women in extradomestic affairs would certainly ruin the happiness of the family and, in the end, would do nothing more than turn women into men.[53] Consequently, according to the Islamic outlook, beyond the exercise of positive law, there exist further limitations, held by the Sharia, concerning the regulation of freedom. The principle of veiling could be cited initially among these religious limitations. Disobedience to this religious rule was assumed by the traditionalists to result in social chaos, and at the same time, to be an act of insubordination to the Islamic order itself. Interestingly enough, the Islamic movement traces the sources of these limitations to the constitution as well. For them the official religion of the Ottoman state was Islam, as guaranteed by the constitution itself; therefore, it is the responsibility of the constitution to guarantee obedience to Islam.[54]

The Islamists of the Constitutional Period also used the Sharia as the basis for their arguments regarding other social issues. According to the Islamists, polygamous marriages, so prevalent in society, were legitimate, for they are in compliance with natural laws and are beneficial to the institution of family itself. Therefore, any judicial change making it easier for women to obtain the right of divorce would result in the collapse of the family.[55]

Women's participation in these discussions, their inclinations to learn European culture, and their new styles of dress during this era were some of the main reasons for distress among Islamists. For Islamist traditionalists, all these freedoms were signs of a moral breakdown of society and even of "prostitution and indecency." In their writings they brought forward examples of dignified and honorable Muslim women in contrast to unveiled, Westernized, flirtatious women. Some Islamists, however, recognized the right to education for Muslim women as long as it was confined to religious education instead of learning, for example, French, piano, and singing. In his book *Meşrutiyet Hanımları (Women of the Constitution)*, Mehmet Tahir (1861–1924) referred to the degeneration of Turkish women under the impact of the West as follows: "The most defining characteristic of our women, dignity, has been replaced by love of lace and ribbon and of fashion and corsets."[56]

Islamists agreed upon the defense of society against the "moral crisis" represented by the West and strongly criticized the imitation of Western manners. Mehmed Akif (1873–1936), a moderate Islamist, criticized the intrusion of Western manners into traditions and the Ottoman way of life: "imitation of religion, manners, clothes, salutations, speech, in short, imitation of everything, means that every individual of that society indeed is actually an imitation, and that society can never succeed in making up a social gathering, thus, cannot exist."[57] Thus, the imitation of these manners, for Islamists, was worthless in the transformation of civilization and would, in turn, adversely affect society, which depended on religious traditions.

As can be seen, the impact of the West on women was seen as the antithesis of Islamic training, leading, for example, to the extension of relations between men and women in the public sphere, *namahrem* and, thus, to the degeneration of society. Accusing the Constitutionalists of neglecting their responsibility with regard to the "guardianship of the Sharia," Derviş Vahdeti (1870–1909) cited the "gradual abandonment of veiling or opening of *meyhanes* and whorehouses in the name of freedom" as examples of the spreading of European morality in society and further noted that women started to unveil in the name of freedom.[58]

During this period of the Second Constitution, the terms of the debate between modernists and conservatives became clearer. If for the Westernists the unveiling of women and their participation in social life served as prerequisites for a "civilized way of life," for the Islamists only the modesty and virtue of women could guarantee the preservation of traditions and of social integrity. Both intellectually and politically, the fundamental issue was the sexual identity and social position of women. The existing political debate, formed around the question of women, depicted the decisive distinction between Western civilization and Eastern Islam as originating in the specific social organizations of these societies; the conceptualization of differences between the sexes, in turn, stemmed from these organizations. The frontiers between interior and exterior as well as between *mahrem* (private) and *namahrem* (public) were drawn upon the female body, or, to put it differently, it was the visibility or invisibility of women that determined these frontiers. The intersection of the *mahrem* and *namahrem* spheres, at which women were positioned, determined the choice of civilization.

The Ideal Turkish Woman

The Turkist movement (the nationalist movement developed by the Ottoman intellectuals during the Second Constitutional Period and that continued to be influential during the Republican Period), however, attempted to transcend the existing conflict between the Islamic and Westernist movements, aiming to establish a link between Western civilization and national culture. The outstanding representative of the Turkist movement, Ziya Gökalp (1876–1924), intended to develop his suggestions regarding modernization in relation to the existing national traditions, aiming at a synthesis of "Turkization, Islamization, and Civilization."[59] Gökalp differed from Islamists since he did not confine traditions merely to religion. He also suggested a new definition of Westernization, with an emphasis on the preservation of national culture, contrary to the Westernists. He disentangled the problematic Westernization from a dilemma between traditional culture and universal civilization, and he dealt with this issue within the context of a nation-state conceptualization.

Gökalp, who criticized both imitative Westernism and conservative Islamism, set forth the idea of a national culture. He considered national culture as a guardian of national identity and as a securing force for social progress. The notion of nation is defined in regard to cultural elements, in Gökalp's thought, and such an approach enabled him to use this concept to signify the passage to civilization and the preservation of cultural essentials.

In his writings Gökalp distinguished the concept of culture from that of civilization and contended that "societies which are foreign to each other in terms of their cultures and religions may converge in civilization."[60] According to Gökalp, the conservation of cultural essences is in fact the mandatory principle in accomplishing civilization, and attaining European rationalism and science is only possible by preserving Turkish culture. In other words, the Turkish nation would become Westernized insofar as it blends its culture and essential characteristics with contemporary civilization. Drawing upon the ideas of Jean-Jacques Rousseau, Gökalp noted the similarity between protecting nature against civilization and preserving Turkish culture against the adverse effects of Western civilization.[61]

Yet, above all, Gökalp argued that Turkish culture needed to be protected from the deleterious impacts of Islam and the negative effects of Arabic and Persian cultures. As he put it, it is necessary to return to the original sources of culture and to resurrect the pre-Islamic past so as to ensure the constitution of a national culture. Gökalp's intention to return to the past in the construction of the future can also be discerned in his ideas regarding women. According to him, Turkish women held equal status with men in pre-Islamic Turkish societies. This past experience of Turkish society should ease the transition of Turkish women to civilization, and it could also dissuade Turkish women from imitating Western women and help secure the institution of the family.

In his defense of the claim that in pre-Islamic Turkish societies both women and men held equal status, Gökalp even made a provocative statement that "the most significant characteristic of the early Turks is feminism."[62] For him there exist two different structures of religious practices in primitive societies: magic and religion. At this stage of social evolution the systems of religion and magic are distinct from each other, yet they maintain equal significance in society.

According to Gökalp, among early Turks women dominated the world of magic, found in the expression of Shamanism. He further stated that the Turkish Shamans wore women's clothes, had long hair and thin voices, shaved their beards and moustaches, and even got pregnant and gave birth in imitation of women; this, it was thought, enabled them to express their predomination in the world of magic. In contrast, the religious system, Toyonism, could be discerned in the sacred power of men. As Gökalp explained, the equal value assigned to each system led to the legal recognition of equality between women and men. Besides this, the required reference to both Toyonism and Shamanism in every social assignment required the participation of both men and women in social affairs. Furthermore, in this society women were not forced to veil.

In regard to the practice of monogamy in early Turkish society, Gökalp also suggested that women were all utterly "free" in pre-Islamic periods. He believed that early Turkish society women were "amazons," entitled to the attributes of "horsemanship, knighthood, heroism" just as men were, and that they served their society as rulers, wardens of castles, and ambassadors. Among former tribes it was only among the Turks that women were regarded as equal to men and received respect. This difference, for Gökalp, and the nonegalitarian relationship between the sexes among non-Turkish tribes resulted from their devaluation of magic.

According to Gökalp, religions that differentiate between magic and religion are the "ascetic" (based on self-denial as a measure of spiritual discipline) ones that treat women as a secondary class. Nevertheless, with the early Turks, equality between men and women indeed sprang from the nature of the prevailing religious system, which could be defined as an "ecstatic" religion (based on spiritual love) that valued both magic and women. Basing his argument on these premises, he claimed that the emergence of ascetic as well as degrading opinions with regard to women in Turkish society could be traced to the adoption of the Islamic religion and that these opinions dominated society for ages under the impact of Arabic and Persian influences. Distinguishing between "pure Islam" and "degenerated Islam," he turned his attention to the rights of women cited in the Koran, and defended Islam. To him, the negative influences of degenerated Islam were the main cause of backwardness and reliance on the old Turkish traditions and the inequality of the family structure. The segregation of the *haremlik* of women from the *selamlık* of men, upon which the tradition of the "mansion" was established in Ottoman society, and the egalitarian house of the former Turks indeed reflect the relative position of women in both societies.[63]

As Ziya Gökalp has argued, the emergence of a novel outlook in Ottoman society occurred during the Tanzimat Period, which, in fact, caused chaos in the Ottoman value system. The displacement of a dogmatic outlook with a positivist one, the objections raised against the regulation of family and work settings on the basis of religious rules, the increasing visibility of women in public areas through their education and labor, and the rise of democratic ideals that questioned the absolute authority of the ruler epitomized the radical transformation Ottoman society underwent during this period.

Gökalp, in his effort to reconcile Turkish past and Western civilization, claims that ancient magic was resurrected under the name of modern civilization; that is, the very notion of civilization refers to evolved patterns of magic. As with magic, the bounds of civilization are not national but international. Both are oriented toward utilitarian values and thus are opposed to the ascetic understanding of religion and morality. Consequently, they both provide equal status for men and women.

For Gökalp, the increasing preponderance of contemporary Western cultural elements in Ottoman society foreshadowed the attainment of equal status for women. The Turkish past thus legitimized the demand for equality of Ottoman women, and it provided the necessary background for this demand.

Gökalp, who utilized "nationalism" as a means to transcend the so-called conflict between Islam and Western civilization, sincerely believed that the essence of civilization was embedded in the "pure essence" of Turkish society. Therefore, along with the birth of the Turkist movement, the underlying cause of the emergence of feminism and populist ideals could be found not only in the values assigned to these by the Western countries of the time but also in the existence of both feminism and democracy in early Turkish society. Above all, he argued, "in the future history will be obliged to confess that both democracy and feminism were born among Turks."[64] Needless to say, such a statement addressed Gökalp's claim that Turks are the founders of civilization, moving beyond the fact that Turkish traditions are compatible with Western civilization. Consequently, Gökalp argued that all nations except for the Turks need to leave their traditions behind in order to enter civilization; all the Turks need to do, however, is to "look into their past."[65]

Visibility and Freedom

The period of the Second Constitution may best be described as the one during which the increasing participation of women in the public sphere, their widespread presence in urban places, the attainment of "social visibility" by women, and objections raised against these developments took place in Ottoman society. During the period of the Second Constitution participation by women in education and the labor force, the establishment of various women's associations, and widespread interest in women's fashions damaged the symbols of women's private realm, such as veiling, the segregation of the sexes, and so on. Consequently, the more women moved beyond the limits of the *mahrem* sphere, the more the state exercised power over them in order to regulate their public life through orders issued and even some regulations enforced by the police.[66]

Around 1919, segregation of men and women within the educational system was abolished, both female and male university students enrolled in the same courses, and, for the first time, Muslim women even joined the

cast of the Istanbul Theater.[67] During this period women actively participated in the organization of various associations, including charity associations and those that aimed at attaining equality between men and women
(e.g., Müdafaa-i Hukuk-i Nisvan) and the right to work (e.g., Osmanlı
Kadınları Çalıştırma Cemiyet-i Islamiyesi).[68] Among these associations,
Müdafaa-i Hukuk-u Nisvan protested against the telephone company
when it refused to recruit female workers, and it was also this association
that dealt with the case of a woman who was not allowed to board a plane
because of her sex.[69]

The more women participated in social life and attained "visibility" in
urban scenes, the more they caused public distress; in turn, issues related
to women acquired greater political meaning. In the meantime ordinary
urban life continued to exercise limits upon the level of companionship
between the sexes; there were special quarters and spaces segregated for
women only in public transportation, such as on streetcars, and in cinemas,
theaters, and restaurants.[70] Nevertheless, at the same time, social traditions
were breaking down. Women who restyled their outdoor garments in the
European fashion started to be seen in the company of their husbands in
the streets and in phaetons; they even "addressed men" in public. Yet,
opposing the "Europeanization" of women, the conservatives adopted
much harsher attitudes toward them. The *imams* (located in big cities such
as Istanbul, Izmir, and Aydin after the declaration of the Second Constitution in 1908) even regarded it as a "requirement of religion" to mistreat
unveiled women, by spitting in their faces in public, for example, or ston-
ing their phaetons.[71] To cite an example, the authorities of Aydin province
(in 1908) province started to exercise severe rules against those who were
caught talking to women in public; the fine for men was one hundred
kuruş, while the women were sentenced to bastinado.[72]

A good example of these attitudes can be seen in a poster printed by
the police in Istanbul in 1917. The poster read:

> In recent months, examples of some disgraceful fashions have been
> observed in the streets of the capital. Thus, all Muslim women are
> asked to lengthen their skirts, wear *charshafs* and not to have corsets.
> They are asked to obey this regulation within two days at most.[73]

Interestingly enough, this poster could not resist the growing will of the
public toward Europeanization, and in response to objections, the authorities issued a new regulation:

The General Administrative Body would like to express its sincere grief aroused upon the declaration of a regulation as a consequence of the persuasion of a low-ranking clerk by old reactionary women, which asked all Muslim women to return to the old fashion. Hereafter we would like to state the outlawing of the recent regulation.[74]

It was urban women especially who halted the traditional practice of segregating the sexes through fashion, entertainment, education and labor. As a consequence, they attained visibility both in terms of the clothes they wore and the space they occupied, along with the notoriety of their exit from the *mahrem* sphere. The objections raised against the "European" liberation of women by conservatives, in the meantime, threatened the power of Young Turks (name given to Ottoman dissidents and reformists in exile in European capitals who demanded radical change and freedom and whose ideas gained power in the Second Constitutional period).

It seems reasonable to conclude this discussion of the pre-Kemalist period by referring once again to the observations of Princess Seniha Sultan. In a letter, written in 1910 in an ironic style, she expressed the difficulties experienced during the adoption of Western styles in the Muslim Ottoman society:

> You ask me to give a detailed account of our current harem life, too, that is, the altered, modernized, recently formed life we have experienced since the revolution. . . . The feminist movement is also among the issues about which you inquire. I write all these sentences with your own words, of course. You have used such words that I rarely use. I can't even deny that I hardly comprehended the meaning of some.[75]

In her letters Seniha wrote that none of the customs and traditions concerning women had changed, despite the high expectations for the revolution among the Young Turks:

> Ah, ah, you assumed many benefits for Turkish women after the reign of Abdülhamid, didn't you? There is no change, my beloved one! . . . As for the feminist Turks, you can only dream this for a long time, my dear.[76]

She even claimed that conditions for women were worse than during the period of Abdülhamid:

Ah my dear sister, I can't forget. . . . It was only a year ago you mentioned that the feminist movement would spring up in Turkey as well. . . . Do you know the conditions today? Look: a Muslim woman is not allowed to get in an "open" car regardless of how many veils she puts on. The roof of the landau and the curtains in the car must be all closed. We have not experienced this during the reign of Abdül-hamid.[77]

Finally, she refers to the feminism of the Young Turks sarcastically:

My young servant, Fatma, has just arrived and gave an item of feminist news to me. Selim Bey's sister—you met him when he was a minister in the old regime—was sentenced to three years by the martial court, and you know why? She unveiled and drank a glass of wine in the Covered Bazaar. . . . Well, what was it I was talking about? Yes, the movement of liberation is in progress.[78]

In a Muslim country, women's adoption of western manners and her visibility in the urban public spaces does not take place smoothly. Women's choices of spaces, manners, and lifestyles trigger a societal and political debate.

Modernity and Veiling

In conjunction with the orientation toward the West and Westernization movements, the question of women was located at the center of political power struggles as well as of discussions taking place between progressives and traditionalists. Beyond the issues of the encounter of the East with the West and of the forms of government (such as Constitutionalism-Oriental despotism), the question of women indeed penetrated the patterns of daily life in Ottoman society. Westernization began to dissolve social patterns determined by Islam, resulting in the reregulation of social space and relations between men and women. So long as the Islamic East lagged behind the rationalist world of the West, its history reflected the influence of Western experiences. That is, upon recognizing the impact of the West on Ottoman consciousness since the Tanzimat Period, all political movements (including Islamic, Westernist, and Turkist ones) have reconsidered their premises in the light of interactions with the West. The "West" is indeed in part an artifact of the Eastern world, rather than a simple reality in itself.

The East has reviewed its own identity in light of Western standards and goals. The more it recognizes the superiority of the West, the more it loses confidence in its own specific identity and history, on the one hand, and, paradoxically enough, the more it seeks its particularistic identity in order to fortify itself against the West, on the other. To quote D. Shayegan (a contemporary Iranian philosopher), in the case of non-Western societies, their "consciousness is wounded."[79] Societies that cannot recognize themselves in their own history are alienated not only from their own praxis but from the "present time" as well. To escape from the reminders of present backwardness, they either seek to return to a mystified Golden Age of the past or to find the path of progress in a utopian future. Within this framework the past and the future are idealized by these societies, while the present time is seen as a "burden. " The word *modernity* acquires a new meaning in societies in which historicity is weak to the extent that it refers constantly to the obsession of "becoming" like the contemporary West, to the fetishistic idea of progress. This can be discerned also in the language itself, in which *modernization* is used interchangeably for *modernity* and *Westernization* for West. If Western modernity and progress are constructed on the idealization of the present time, a wish to escape to the future or the past is a defining attribute of societies with weak historicity.

Islamic movements are no exception. They have not developed independently of the ideal of progress, the question of alienation, and the projection of Western superiority. According to Ismail Kara (a contemporary Islamist writer), Islamists lost their self-confidence because of the material and technical superiority of the Western world, and this is the main reason that they became dependent on the "ideal of progress, the outcome of evolutionist thinking itself," instead of turning back to the sources for *"tecdit"* (renovation).[80] He even argues that the Islamists found themselves in a "defensive position" against Western civilization and then adopted various slogans, including: "Islam does not hinder progress," and "Muslims misinterpret Islam," "Civilization and Islam are not antithetical to each other," and "Western technological civilization must be adopted if necessary."[81]

Nevertheless, the social organization established on the basis of *mahremiyet* (privacy) and hierarchical relations, was subject to dissolution in the face of Western principles of equality and liberation. In order to comprehend the changes taking place at the level of everyday life and the collective imagination, the essence and dynamics of the Western cultural model need to be defined with reference to the equality principle, as elaborated by Tocqueville. The development of Western societies is dependent upon the principle of equality between races, citizens, classes, and the sexes. This, of course, does not mean that, in reality, equality is totally achieved. What is important here is that history has evolved in reference to this principle. Democracy is fueled by the "passion for equality," the egalitarian ideology, rather than by the phenomenon of equality.[82] In other words, society aims to transcend and change itself depending upon egalitarian utopias. The idea of equality between women and men as well as the ideal of the attainment of the status of human beings for women are all aspects of the process of equalization.[83] The second principle of the Western cultural model refers to the unfolding process of the transparency of private life as an outcome of liberal philosophy. In other words, in Western societies certain issues that concern families and individuals, issues of the private sphere, are increasingly brought into the public sphere. In line with this transparency, as Foucault has argued, discursive sexuality is not repressed; on the contrary, it is constantly provoked.[84] For Foucault, Western civilization, constructed upon a scenario of "confession," tries to verbalize explicitly every possible intimate and private affair. Justice, medicine, familial relations, and daily life fall into the sphere of confession and guilt; illness, sin, desire, and other problems are all confessed.[85] The culture of Islam, on the other hand, is established not only on the invisibility of the *mahrem* sphere and of women but also on the "secrecy" and "nonverbalization" of the affairs taking place in the *mahrem* realm; it is a society of silence, thus, it is antiliberal by its very organization. The veiling of women, indicative of the private sphere and a culture of secrecy, therefore, illustrates the existing asymmetry between Islamic and Western societies and their distinct organization of life spaces and lifestyles.

This is exactly why the increasing visibility of women and the emergence of the private sphere act as the touchstone of Westernization. Women's place thus defines, on the one hand, the degree of orientation toward Western civilization and, on the other, the degree to which the Muslim community is preserved. The practice of veiling, for Westernists, is the main obstacle to modernization; for the Islamists, it is the leading symbolic force against the degeneration of society.

Islamists recognize the possibility of importing the technological advancements of the West, yet they object to any adoption of the "customes and morality as well as lifestyle" of the West. Social morality is defined by religious rules, and it operates mainly upon the regulation of women's sexuality. The preservation of honor—that is, loyalty to moral codes in relation to women's sexuality—is a necessary condition of the social order. Since women's sexuality is regarded as a threat (*fitne*) to the social order, women must be isolated from men and covered by veils.

The basic premise of the Islamic outlook may be summarized as follows: veiling is a social requirement. The honor of a woman is directly proportional to the distance she is away from "abuse," or the possibility of sexual harassment. It is veiling itself that ensures the required distance. A look invites lust and causes sedition; a lustful gaze leads to an illicit act (*haram*); and it is illicit to look at a woman if her clothes cling to her body. The emergence of women into the outside world depends upon certain rules. Cohabitation of women and men is forbidden, for it is among the reasons for the increase in cases of adultery (flirtation). It is forbidden also for a woman to stay alone with a man (*halvet*) who is not a family member because it is a possible sin and a possible imputation against her honor. It is only proper to shake a woman's hand when she is old enough to be "delivered from lust."[86]

Opposing this, Westernists wanted to institute the "New Life," and they favored a "social revolution" only after the "political one."[87] The main criterion of the New Life was the emancipation of women from the traditional way of life and their consequent participation in social life. During the Constitutional Period the position of women was the fundamental criterion of a change in civilization, and they were regarded as the leaders of the New Life. Among the statements commonly heard were the following: "In times of freedom half of society cannot be imprisoned"; "Women should participate in social life through their labor"; "The future of society is dependent upon the progress of women"; and "Women act as the criterion of civilization."[88]

Westernism is, in a sense, to quote Peyami Safa (1899–1961), "the yearning for progress which springs from the need for civilization against religious bigotry."[89] The ideal of progress targets Safa's traditional communitarian values, which were based upon the invisibility of women. Safa's article "The Dream of a Westernist" depicts a civilized world, free of religious conservatism, in which women can dress the way they wish, police and religious men do not intervene in the clothing habits of women, women are respected by men as the main benefactors of the country, women and girls do not run away from men, and, finally, the practice of arranged marriages is not followed.[90]

Nevertheless, the orientation toward the West did not follow a defined course; the boundaries of modernism are continuously being redrawn. In the words of Taner Timur (contemporary social scientist), the Ottomans, unaware of the social transformation they were experiencing, tried to act and think in a European manner while, concurrently, they were antipathetic toward the West.[91] Safa drew attention to the fact that the "cosmopolitanism" associated with Europeanization was criticized persistently; Turkists clung to nationalist aspects of traditions, while Islamists clung to religious ones.[92]

Following the Tanzimat Period the "moderns" idealized the West as the source of freedom, beauty, and the world of art; for the youngsters of the new generation Europe represented the "Life of Imagery."[93] In the meantime, however, the yearning for Europeanization became a subject for ridicule; modernism was equated with the alienation of "pseudo-intellectuals" from the public. Ahmet Mithad Efendi (1844–1912), who criticized the unrestrained adoption of Western culture, and who depicted the first of a "snobbish Westernized type" in his novels, referred to modernists as "decadents," alienated and uprooted people.[94] Celal Nuri (1881–1938), too, criticized the imitation of the West claiming that "Western civilization, which has been sold particularly to Turkish girls of high society, has entered society without any rules and manners" and has created "socially outrageous people."[95]

A determined defender of Western civilization, Salahaddin Asim, too, targeted women of the so-called upper class for appropriating the European way of life. In *The Upper-Class Woman, Life, and Womanization* he argued that women of this class live "outside intelligence and civilization," that "they only sit and talk." He depicted the members of this class as superficial, formalistic and idle, as follows:

> For us, upper-class life means having more and better food, cruising in a car, riding a horse, wandering around Şehvet Harmani at Fener, idling in summer houses, having a piano or a violin at home and trying to play them, furnishing rooms with ornate and pompous furniture; that, in short, it is pretentiousness.

Women who fancy European freedom have chosen the "freedom of pleasure and indecency" instead of the "freedom of working like men in society." For him "the European lifestyle of these women" is nothing but the "upper-class version of womanization." The only difference between women of elite circles and others is that the former have had a "cosmopolitan" lifestyle while the latter have had a "national" lifestyle.[96]

The religious and moral rules of the Islamists, which served to protect the community, were displaced by the "good manners" of the Westernists. The communitarian norms resisted well the cosmopolitanism of Europeanization. Şerif Mardin even argues that the character of Bihruz Bey in Recaizade Ekrem's novel *Araba Sevdasi*, which depicts the ultra-Westernization of society at that particular time, is the key to comprehending anticosmopolitan inclinations in Turkish history. The character of Bihruz Bey, a spoiled son of a pasha, admirer of the West, and an ill-mannered person, illustrated the superficiality and similarly ridiculous aspects of cosmopolitanism. For Mardin the anti-Bihruz syndrome expresses traditional communitarian norms against such "ultramodernism."

Along with its radical Westernism the republican nationalism, too, has certain anticosmopolitan characteristics within its populist and nationalist discourses.[97] In preparing a course of action for Kemalists, the Turkist movement tried to lay down a frontier drawn by Turkish "national identity and manners" against the extremes of Westernism and Islamism. Claiming that "Turkhood is the real fulcrum of Islam and Ottomanhood against cosmopolitanism" and that "the manners of Tanzimat have corrupted as well," Ziya Gökalp suggested "a new manner" for the New Life.[98] The enterprise of civilization thus acquired a new dimension, a national one, and the themes of populism and nationalism were emphasized, in contrast to the cosmopolitanism of the Western-influenced Ottoman period.

The New Life was to be based upon "national family" and "national manners" for Turkists, who were indeed in pursuit of a national identity. Gökalp's words, "Let my country be prosperous and my home fortunate," expressed this sense of identification with the ideals of family and nation. The institution of family, established on conventional relationships, became the target of new ideals and entered into the world of change. Stating that "We Turks do not know family life. A person ought to take his/her family into account after the nation; he or she must work for the family after his/her country," Gökalp took the institution of family into the sphere of national ideals, with a moralistic attitude.[99] Thus according to Zafer Toprak, the family, which had been confined to the private sphere up to that time, was brought into public life and redefined with the guidance of new national norms.[100] As much as the liberation of the family, women, too, were not exposed to public debates, and their "socialization" was supported as a national issue. The emancipation of women for such honorable reasons as making them part of the national family, or the nation itself, would not contradict the virtues of womanhood. Women would no longer be defined as babydolls, consumers of the West, or the causes of subversive acts; rather, stripping off their former sexual identity, they would serve their nation for "the people," as the "companions" of men. Thus, women would have the status of "beneficial human beings." Women's visibility and sociability is associated with the image of women who are educated and who are serving their nation, rather than concerned with "pleasure."

The very best example of this new image of women is to be found in the works and life of Halide Edip Adıvar (1882–1964). The female characters in her novels, written under the influence of nationalism, are significantly different from the women of Ottoman households, with their ordinary shoes, gray coats, white headcovers, and bags in their hands—especially in their desire to work for their country. The "Yeni Turan" women of Adıvar's fiction were no longer the "decorative elements of their houses" and "sources of love for their husbands" but were teachers and nurses and were all "dignified," "beneficial, hardworking members of society," and "sincere companions of men and mothers of the whole nation."[101]

Adıvar, in fact, drew the ideal type of Kemalist women: those who aim to serve the nation, who are participants in political affairs. At the same time they do not lack "tenderness"; they are dignified companions, mothers of the nation, populists. Of a female character in *Yeni Turan*, she wrote that "there was no sign recalling either sex, neither male nor female, in this [her] look"; moreover, the woman is not even intentionally beautiful, but she is strong and struggles for the benefit of her nation. The dignified female characters are close to the common people—very modest in their physical outlook and virtually lacking femininity; they are the messengers of the coming republican women.

CHAPTER 3

Kemalism:
The Civilizing Mission

Beyond its success in the transformation of the state structure from an Islamic empire to a secular nation-state, Kemalism, indeed, was the most conscious expression of the civilizational shift experienced by Turkish society since the Tanzimat Period, penetrating daily family life.[1] Stating that society had "entered into the circle of a secular civilization," Ziya Gökalp recognized three distinct "circles of civilization" through which Turkish people had passed during three different stages of their history. The Turks decided to be part of the Far East during the period of the ethnic state, to be part of Eastern civilization during the period of the empire, and to be part of Western civilization with the decision to be a nation-state.[2] The transition to Western civilization affected manners, clothing, the use of space, and the rhythm of daily life. Peyami Safa has suggested that "the duality which sets at loggerheads the furnishings of the house and clothing in fact originated from the painful process of the preference between the Islamic East and the Christian West," and it is Kemalism itself that halted this duality.[3]

The authors of the early Republican Period were entangled in the dualism of East and West, and sought to decipher the impact of this dualism on the Turkish people and their history. One author of the period, Ahmet Hamdi Tanpınar (1901–1962), defined this dualism, the encounter of two distinct worlds in daily life, as "the tragedy of the current Turkish spirit," further maintaining that "we have moved towards the West with a will reinforced by the requirements of the history, yet at the same time, we own a past such that it is impossible to close our ears once it starts to talk to us with all its quality." For him Westernization should be seen as more than a conflict between the new and the old—rather, as the "illness of civilizational change," and even a "psychosis," which settled inside the Turks and which concerns the "inner self." Admitting that the chain of continuity with the past had been broken since the Tanzimat Period and that the past itself had turned into an "almost dead form of life still living inside us,"

Tanpınar hoped for the end of life that is placed "at a knot, in the middle of the two different but overlapping worlds, unaware of each other" and for the "sealing of the chain of continuity inside ourselves" in the Republican Period.[4]

With the onset of the Republican Period it was hoped that the question of East-West duality would be transcended with the conceptualization of a new nation, a new civilization, and a new future. The Istanbul correspondent of *Le Temps* newspaper, Paul Gentizon, highlighted this rupture of society in 1929 when he wrote: "The Turkish Republic cut its umbilical cord ties with Asian traditions, accepted the mentality and ideals of Western civilization, and thus, said farewell to the East."[5]

Thus, the Kemalist reforms attempted to penetrate into the lifestyle, manners, behavior and daily customs of the Turkish people, beyond the transformation of the state apparatus. Admitting the difficulties of Turkish people in experiencing "the West," Paul Dumont depicted this phenomenon as follows:

> They ought to give up the Eastern clothes; the turban, fez, shalwar, sandals, thin veils; they have to stop practising polygamy, they must leave aside the Arabic alphabet and writing incomprehensible amulets with these letters, they should stop measuring time with the sun, they must change their weight and length measures, their life styles, frames of mind and their perspective on life."[6]

Although the concept of "civilization" refers to a wide range of themes, from the level of technology to customs of eating and drinking, as pointed out by Norbert Elias, it refers initially to the "expression of the Western consciousness," the "national feeling of the West." In short, it is the expression of the superiority of the West. It provides a summary of the phenomena that make the West distinctive from other social styles, due to its own specific experiences, 'proud', and original, in the face of other contemporary yet "primitive" societies: technology, rules of decent manners, worldview, and everything else.[7] In other words, the concept of civilization defines the superiority of the West and attributes universality to its own cultural model.

Nevertheless, Western culture and civilization do not constitute a monolithic entity. According to Elias, the identification between civilization and culture, basically formed by the French and English experiences, acquired a different meaning in the history of Germany, where the national characteristics of culture gained significance. The notion of "culture" in German is the expression of "specificity" underlying national differences. French and English notions of "civilization" however, with their universalist orientations, are indifferent to the existing differences between nations and people. Civilization is the ideal to be attained, it is the future rather than the past. It is progressive in nature. The French and English comprehension of civilization fundamentally deals with the styles of human behavior. This is the reason why a cultivated (*cultivé*), "enlightened/intellectual" person is associated with the characteristics of a "civilized" person. To put it differently, social customs and manners, degrees of urbaneness, use of language, household life, manner of dress, and style of salutation are open to scrutiny. Therefore, the description of a person as "cultivated" does not bring to mind the cultural works of that person but, rather, it recalls his or her degree of conformity with social customs and manners. Norbert Elias has suggested that the distinction between the French concept of "civilization" and German concept of "culture" originates from the operation of distinct relations between the social classes and political power in these societies. For instance, in contrast with the French and English experiences, the intellectuals and bourgeoisie of Germany could not penetrate the aristocracy ("society"), and they supported the distinctiveness of the German language and culture against the court, while, in the meantime, the aristocracy of Germany adapted French language, literature, and manners. For the intellectuals German culture is representative of "depth" and "the real virtues" in contrast to the "superficiality," "snobbery," and "excessive interest in ceremony" that have been identified with French culture. Given these facts, Elias argued that German nationalism indeed speaks for the new ideals of the rising middle class and the bourgeoisie; the defining characteristics of this class would become the national characteristics of Germans once they came to power.[8]

It is reasonable to assume that the Turkish Kemalist movement embodied both German nationalism and French universalism. Peyami Safa has stated that there exist two constant principles of Atatürk's revolution: Nationalism and Civilization.[9] The concept of civilization directed the route to Westernization toward France. After the Tanzimat Period the Western style of clothes and way of life were among the main interests of the Ottomans. Caricatures published even before the republic focused upon the distinction between "civilization and barbarism," and they ridiculed changing habits of dress and household articles. In these caricatures divans, tobacco pipes, and light thin-soled boots were the "signs of

barbarism," while tight-waisted, baloon-skirted clothes, bowler hats, walking sticks, tables, and French grammar books were the "tools of civilization."[10] It had been possible to witness European fashion since the reign of
Mahmud II, when slit-sleeved stout jackets, robes, and gowns were
replaced with frock coats designed in the European style, while *shalwar*
(Turkish trousers) and knee-breeches worn with tight leggings were
replaced by trousers. It was even the case that, during the Crimean War,
Sultan Abdülmecid asked all his clerks to wear frock coats, which was
mentioned later in the well-known "Katibim" song.[11]

Abdülmecid (1823–1861) was also the first sultan to order the women
of his harem to wear European corsets at a circumcision ceremony.[12] With
the coming republican period, however, the Occidental way of life represented the symbols of civilization to be attained and was incorporated into
official ideology. Wearing neckties, shaving beards and moustaches, going
to the theater, eating with a fork, exercising, the practice of husbands and
wives walking hand in hand in the streets, dancing at balls, shaking hands,
wearing hats in the street, and writing from left to right were among the rituals that defined a progressivist, civilized, and ideal republican individual.
Cevdet Kudret, in his article *"Alafranga Dedikleri" (What They Call Occidental)*, acknowledges that what was regarded as occidental, which had been
ridiculed in literary works since the Tanzimat Period because of its imitative content and referred to as "snobbish, chic, civilized, *bopstil* [dandy],"
was now an integral part of daily life, throughout rural as well as urban settlements. Thus, the occidental way of life almost defeated the oriental
one.[13]

It can be seen that the official ideology of the republic does not differentiate its utopia of civilization from lifestyles and clothing habits. Stating
that "The people of the Turkish Republic, which acknowledges civilization,
ought to prove their state of civilization with their family life, lifestyle, and
their outer appearance from head to foot," Mustafa Kemal pointed out the
significance of clothing in the process of Westernization with the enactment
of the "hat reform":

> Civilized and international clothes are the ones which our precious
> nation deserves. Shoes for ladies and half-boots for men, trousers,
> waistcoats, shirts, ties, collars and, naturally, complementary to all
> these, sun-protective head-covering. As a matter of fact, this is called a
> "hat."[14]

Consequently, in 1925 a special law on the hat, which was assumed to convey significant importance for a Turkey determined to be part of the union of contemporary nations, was introduced into society as a symbol of Westernization.

Underlining the "universal" characteristics and "international" recognition of Western clothes, Kemal suggested that the clothing habits of the Ottomans, including the fez and the robe, actually originated in the cultures of non-Muslim and even "hostile" nations, testing their possible rejection by society: "If it is permissible to wear the Greek head-covering, the fez, why should not the hat be allowed? Once again I want to ask them and the whole nation how and why they wore the special clothing of the Byzantine priests and Jewish rabbis, the robe?"[15]

Although it cannot be argued that the conventional clothing habits could be traced back to Islam, the extensive concern over the clothing reforms in fact stemmed from the "religious and traditional" significance attributed to both fez and *charshaf* (veiling).[16] Kemal ended the identification of the Turks with the Ottomans through his implementation of the hat reform. As Ernest Jackh stated "Atatürk uprooted the Turks from Ottomanhood with the abandonment of ordinary caps and fezzes."[17] The acceptance of the hat, as representative of Western civilization, in place of the fez, the symbol of identification with Ottomanhood and the eradicator of all national differences, prepared the ground for the abandonment of veiling. Deserting the Ottoman identity by welcoming the hat, the Turks further extended the boundaries of *mahrem*, predetermined by the religious authorities and Sharia, by abandoning the practice of veiling.

Kemal himself reinforced the companionship of men and women. For instance, at a reception organized in 1924 on the anniversary of the republic's founding, to which diplomats and top-level bureaucrats were invited, Kemal observed that none of the female guests had danced. He kindly asked them to join in the dancing saying: "My friends, I cannot imagine any woman in the world who would refuse a Turkish officer's invitation to dance. I now order you: spread out through the dance hall! Forward! March! Dance!"[18]

For Tarık Zafer Tunaya, Mustafa Kemal (or Atatürk), who declared a war against the "oriental mentality," regardless of whether or not he would be left alone in this war, was the "outstanding defender of the civilization concept," and Kemal aimed to sort out the duality between culture and civilization taking place in society since the Tanzimat Period, on behalf of the republic and of civilization. For this reason Atatürk suggested a "national renaissance," to use the terminology of Tunaya, in contrast to the "Islamic renaissance" proposals.[19]

As far as the principle of nationalism was concerned, it fundamentally relied upon the populism of Anatolia in opposition to the elitist cosmopolitanism of the Ottomans. It indeed designated the coming to power of the rising middle class, as illustrated in the German nationalist case by Elias. As the ideology of "civilization/westernization" corresponded to the superiority of the West in terms of the encounter between the East and the West, nationalism stood for the victory of the new bureaucratic elites over the court in the power relations of the political classes. In short, with the help of Kemalism it was the advent of the "bureaucratic tradition," termed "the right wing" by İdris Küçükömer, that can be detected in the rising of the "Westernist-civilized-secularist" movement to power since the Union of Progress and Order (a political organization that governed the Ottoman state overall during the Second Constitutional Period from 1908 to 1918).[20] In contrast to Ottoman cosmopolitanism and the elites of the court, the Kemalist nationalism expressed the rise of the bureaucratic middle classes through its exaltation of Anatolia and the War of Independence. It was against the court in orientation, yet it assumed the Westernist inclinations of the court. In other words, being distinct from German bourgeois nationalism, it was not built upon the originality of the national/local culture in contrast to civilization. It was the discursive meltingpot of Anatolian populism and Westernist elitism. Along these lines François Georgeon maintains that it was the "populist" and "romantic" nationalism of Ziya Gökalp rather than the bourgeois nationalism of Yusuf Akçura that addressed the aspirations of the petit bourgeoisie and the bureaucratic aspects of Turkish society.[21] Hence, Turkish nationalism was backed by the discourse of populism instead of the originality of national cultural works. "Toward the People" and "Going to the People" were the main slogans of the nationalist movement, and the "glorification of the nation" was identified with the "glorification of the people."[22]

Westernist attitudes about civilization, however, and the attempts of the nationalist ideology to appear rooted in Anatolia seem to embody a potential conflict. How would it be possible to articulate Westernization, aiming at the abandonment of "Alaturka" (the Turkish style, used to express the way foreigners look at Turks), with the ideology of nationalism, seeking its legitimacy in Anatolia? The process of civilization, in a sense, uprooted the nationalist ideology from its cultural sources. As can be witnessed in the mentality of Ziya Gökalp as well, Turkish nationalism was intended to be free from the impacts of Islam and traces its sources back to the pure and imaginary Turkish culture of the past. This imaginary Turkish culture served, on the one hand, the rediscovery of the Turkish identity, buried because of Ottomanism, by the collective consciousness and, on the other hand, the expression of compatibility of the Turks with Western culture. Its basic attributes are bound up with the designation of the existence of a Turkish nation as against the prevalent Ottomanism as well as the inclusion of the Turkish nation within the sphere of civilization. Not only Gökalp's claim that "the most significant characteristic of early Turks is feminism" but also the linguistic and historical theories of Mustafa Kemal, "The Theory of Sun-Language" and "The Thesis of Turkish History," respectively, both of which aim to prove that it is the Turkish language and history from which Asiatic languages and nations descend, sought to show the congruency of the Golden Age of the Turks with Western civilization. And, above all, what they aim to show is that the former does not differ from the latter whatsoever. Turkish nationalism seeks ground for the detachment of the rising bureaucracy from the Ottomans and for the concurrent yearnings for identification with the West. With the disappearance of the question of Ottomanism with time, Kemalist nationalism became the main defender of the unitary Turkish nation-state. This is exactly why it is beyond mere coincidence that the nationalist movements, which fundamentally address inherent culture and traditions, spring generally from among rightist movements and ideologies.

Anatolian Women and the Western Way of Life

The Kemalist approach to the question of women seems to offer an invaluable opportunity for explication, for it may throw light upon the duality between civilization and nationalism. The main reason for this comes from the fact that it was the women upon whom the Kemalist movement relied with respect to both the process of modernization and the ideology of nationalism. In a sense it was the women who were the standard-bearers of Kemalist reforms. As asserted by Şirin Tekeli, Kemalist women's rights were the symbolic democratization efforts of the state in answer to the accusations about dictatorship by the Western world. Nevertheless, the word *symbolic* here does not mean "insignificant." On the contrary, so long as women's rights are related to the exercise of secularism in a Muslim country, they are loaded with political meaning, and, thus, "there exists a dialectical relationship between struggles for women's rights and struggles directed toward the eradication of the effectiveness of religion."[23] The political rights granted to women "play a symbolic role in the determination of the definition of the regime," beyond its significance from the point of view of women.[24]

The question of women did not emerge as a secondary issue on the agenda of Kemalism, but, rather, it enables us to comprehend the essence of this ideology. The Kemalist movement acted as a protector of the principle of secularism at the expense of democracy. The leading indicator of the principle of secularism, however, was the importance attributed to women's rights in a Muslim country. Nonetheless, the affinity between secularism and women's rights does not operate solely within the political sphere as the designation of the formation of a secular state; rather, it carves out the patterns of daily life. As depicted previously, since the Tanzimat Period the question of women accompanied the advancement of "civilization consciousness," and with the onset of the republican era women became leading actors in the civilizational change. Anatolian women represented this change and the formation of a national consciousness directed toward Western civilization. In contrast to Ottoman women, who were considered coquettish and alienated from their people, and Muslim women who were considered to be subordinated by religion and alienated from progress, Anatolian women were brought onto the scene as main figures. Just as populism supported Kemalist nationalism, the Kemalist women's movement glorified Anatolian women in contrast to Ottoman cosmopolitanism. The attributes of Anatolian women, accentuated in the discourses of Mustafa Kemal, still lie in the collective Turkish memory: "It is always they, the noble, self-sacrificing, godly Anatolian women who plough, cultivate the land, fell firewood in the forest, barter in the marketplace and run the family; and above all, it is still they who carry the ammunition to the front on their shoulders, with their ox-carts, with their children, regardless of rain, winter and hot days."[25] Anatolian women were both the "savers" and the "saved" ones: they were expected to save the republican reforms from "degeneration," while these reforms, in turn, saved them from the fanaticism of Islam. Thus, Kemalist women served as a bridge between civilization and nation.

Meanwhile, the concept of civilization brought a sharp distinction between the "civilized" and "uncivilized" onto the scene. Although scientific knowledge, the opera, new habits of cuisine, Western-style furniture, and other such preferences symbolically represented Western civilization, once again issues concerning male and female relations were the most disputed ones. The clothing of men and women (veils, hats, etc.), the determination of space allocation for the sexes, and the regulation of relations between the sexes were the focus of attention and the starting point of civilization. This is exactly why the position of women in society was the touchstone of Kemalist civilization. As we have witnessed in discussions taking place since the Tanzimat Period, the emergence of women from the private, closed familial space into the outer world, the shrinkage of the *mahrem* sphere, the increasing visibility of women, and their companionship with men were the fundamental points of divergence between traditionalist Islamists and supporters of Westernist reforms. Although traditionalism, Islamism, reformism, and Westernism all changed and acquired new meanings through the course of time, the "question of women" as the main point of divergence between them remained unchanged. As a matter of fact, in the post-1980s period the woman question reemerged as the main cause of dispute between the radical Islamist movement and the supporters of secularism.

The visibility of women in the urban arena and their companionship with men beyond the confinements of "isolation" and segregation, the organization of dances, visits to confectioners' shops in the early evenings, riding horses, and similar "foreign" customs were all appreciated and constituted the new features of the early republic. The definitions and divisions between the civilized and primitive and the progressivist and reactionary were continuosly held. Since Oriental *(Alaturka)* manners and habits were classified as "primitive" and "reactionary," conformity to the "civilized way of life" was among the requirements for a distinct social status and privilege. To cite an example, the conjugal visits of wives and husbands as families, to use the popular term of those years, was regarded as a civilized custom, whereas those who were against this were assumed to be "traditionalist reactionaries." As observed by an early sociologist of the republican period, Muhaddere Taşçıoğlu, there were some men who went to the "reception days" of some women in the company of their wives so as to get rid of the "reactionary" label; thus, it was even possible to see a single man at some of the receptions held by women.[26]

During the early Republican era, the impacts of Westernization started to be seen in the Turkish collective conscience, yet this was restricted to a small group of urbane people. Both women and men started to adjust their behavior in accordance with the image of an idealized European person. "Here we have men and women sitting again separately" is among the sentences often used up to the present time, and it certainly designates the desire and the efforts of Turkish people to exercise control upon their *"alla turca"* behavior.

In the meantime the distinction between civilized and uncivilized began to influence the values attributed to aesthetics as well, and sources of the definition of beauty started to be found on the European Continent rather than in the local milieu. The oriental understanding of beauty dependent on whiteness, rounded curves, loose clothing, long hair, henna, and stibium was replaced by "foreign beauty"—slimness, high energy, and the wearing of corsets and short hair. "You look like a European" was a major compliment.[27]

The preferences in beauty moved from "strength, health, and fertility," natural qualities, to "delicacy, elegance, and Western manners," acquired qualities. An article entitled *"Korse Meselesi"* (The Question of the Corset) pointed out the symbolic importance the corset introduced into women's lives in the prerepublican period as well as the changing understanding of beauty in society. It reproached the authors and poets who argued, for instance, as follows: "For what reason do they not regard a mighty, strong and healthy woman as 'beautiful' and look for the art of beauty in complete health, but try to define delicacy and elegance in those pages."[28]

It was indeed the case that the corset formed the female body in accordance with Western criteria. Nora Şeni argues that, as a consequence of the acceptance of the corset, "which is the most important article effective in the determination of the silhouette, elegance, and the uprightness of contemporary Western women," Turkish women would no longer have their previous physical appearance: "The soft, fattish and loose body contours of Eastern women, fancied by Orientalist excursionists and artists . . . were all replaced by an upright posture, 'upright silhouette' of women."[29]

A slim body, narrow hips, small breasts, and an upright posture were all reflections of the new European understanding of aesthetics inspired by urbane and active women who work and spend time with men. Along with their functional diversification—working clothes during the daytime, play clothes in the afternoon; cocktail dresses in the evening; dinner, ballet, or theater clothing at night; sports outfits; and beach, tennis, and riding clothes—women's clothes indicated the increasing participation of European women in the social sphere. For republican elite women, however, fashion seems to reflect the changing taste of the upper classes rather than indicating the changing social status of women.[30]

Nonetheless, the change of taste was not innocent, either. Above all, with its transience, superficiality, and visibility, fashion served as a Trojan horse in the exaltation of a new civilization, a new way of life and behavior patterns. Corsets, trousers, Western-style chairs, gramophones, and other similar goods that entered Turkish life were determining factors in the formation of the new posture, movement, and entertainment habits of the Turks. Georg Simmel acknowledged that it is clothing itself that directly determines the tempo of walking, stature, and gestures of a person; thus, similar clothing habits result in similar patterns of behavior.[31] Turkish people in pursuit of European fashion also tried to internalize related behavior patterns that are an integral part of Western civilization; nonetheless, the Turkish body remained uncomfortable in its adjustment to the requirements of this new language: "It was one of the first evening performances in Ankara [in the early 1930s]. At that time nobody knew how to behave appropriately, how to sit, walk, dance, and how to use their hands and head in acting."[32]

The imitation of fashions, which did not spring from local aesthetics, dynamics of class and privileges, also served to promote Western civilization. The trend that introduced Western clothing and ways of life in the face of the ahistorical Muslim clothing habits, defined by their resistance to change, dependence on tradition, expressiveness of ethnic and local differentiations as well as of privilege by virtue of material and jewels, introduced the concept of time, as well as the criterion of modernity, into the monotonous Eastern world. Fashion attributes positive values to change and novelty, sharpening our consciousness with regard to the present time.[33] Its transience does not reduce the value of fashion; on the contrary, this characteristic strengthens it. For fashion heightens the consciousness of modernity, based upon the principles of change and the fetishism of the present time and it fed Kemalist Westernization, subverting the old habits of society and concretizing the new patterns of lifestyles. It created a new *habitus*, to use Bourdieu's term, new social distinctions between social classes.

On the other hand, the consciousness of Kemalist nationalism was wounded by this cultural change. The indulgence of women in fashion became the main target of the criticisms by supporters of Westernism. This indulgence and interest in Western fashion was criticized not only by conservative Islamists but also by nationalists, who were strongly opposed to Ottoman cosmopolitanism.[34] As an outcome of this, the increasing feeling of nationalism among the intellectuals affected the writers of *Kadınlar Dünyası* (The World of Women), who targeted fashion in their articles dur-

ing the years of economic recession and war: "How could we think of fashion in these years when cannonballs and bullets are heard all over the
country? . . . We pay lots of money to foreigners for jewellry and toiletries,
and in turn, they send all this back to us as cannons, rifles, and bullets."[35]

The novel *Ankara* by Yakup Kadri (published in 1934) is among the
best examples of the tension between Westernization and nationalism. The
leading female character in the novel, Selma (interestingly enough, people
in the novel often cannot pronounce this "modern" name well and call her
"Esma"), assumes the character of a "civilized woman" (i.e., Westernized),
and, thus, she is alienated from her people. Yet, she can find her fulfillment
only in her people.

In the first part of the novel she moves from Istanbul to Ankara. She
cannot find the comfort, wealth, and civilization of Istanbul in the rural
town of Ankara; her lifestyle and even her physical appearance create distance between herself and her neighbors, representing the people of Anatolia. Selma, who was depicted as having a fine stature by the vigorous
neighborhood women, yet at the same time as a "boyish person" without
"hips and breasts," represents a different lifestyle: she eats at the same table
with men and rides horses in their company. Nonetheless, the occidental
way of life, represented by the gramophone, Swiss governesses, white
gloves, and dancing and bridge parties, alienates the leading female character of the novel not only from her own people but also from herself. Giving credit to the fact that "the question of nationalism almost turned into
the question of modernity," Yakup Kadri called on his characters to turn
back to the "plain, intimate, and strongly personal, sincere life" experienced during the period of the struggle for national independence:

> Turkish women would have forsaken their *charshafs* and veils to be
> able to work with more ease and comfort. The meaning of participa-
> tion into social life would not have led them to join this sort of social
> gathering. Yes, a Turkish woman should have claimed her freedom
> and used it not to dance and to polish her nails . . . to be a puppet, but
> to undertake a demanding and serious role in the constitution and
> development of a new Turkey. And Turkish men, on the other hand,
> would not have equated the Westernization movement with the pro-
> Westernism and Occidentalism of the Tanzimat men.[36]

The duality between occidental civilization and traditional people
could also be found in the depiction of the dissociation between the elites

and the people, as set forth by the author: on the one hand, the dancing tea parties and, on the other, religious gatherings; on the one hand, Euro-peanized gentlemen who compliment and bow to women with an exagger-ated manner and, on the other, Anatolian men who beat their wives—all portrayed the traps that the degenerating elites and the traditional people fell into. Kadri aimed to sort out this question through the utopia of Ankara. The emancipation of Selma and her "engagement to Ankara and its expres-sion of the national goal" are of equal value.[37] While Istanbul turns into a "center of pleasure and enjoyment, a city of tourism and a cosmopolitan port," with its pompous music halls, luxurious hotels, and bars, Ankara "has become a dull city," for "there existed only symphony concerts in the name of music," while mainly literary and foreign plays were staged at the Halkevi (the People's House).[38] It was the utopia of Ankara, indeed, that brought the intersecting point between the people and civilization into exis-tence. Ankara, the capital of the Republic, brought visual as well as official dimensions into the enterprise of modernization, along with its various buildings, including the Halkevi, the Parliament, the State Theater, and the State Opera and Ballet, and it also embraced the steppes of Anatolia lying far away from Ottoman cosmpolitanism, represented by Istanbul.

A conversation from Yakup Kadri's book that takes place at the New Year's ball organized at the Ankara Palas Hotel throws light on the duality between civilization and populism. To begin with, it was an accepted proposition that the only solution to prevent reforms from degenerating and to avoid losing contact with reality lay in "going to the people." But what does "going to the people" mean exactly? In contrast to the argument of one guest, who stated that "the real meaning of `going to the people' is drawing them towards yourself," another gave credit to "returning to the people," expressing his sincere feelings of alienation from the people:

> While I was climbing up the stairs, I experienced a weird giddiness. I felt as if each stair increased the distance between the people and me . . . Suddenly I found myself in a state of confusion. I lost myself. At that moment, that group of people in the street seemed to me to be the expression of a real entity, more real than myself. The reason for me to return to them appeared at that moment. To find the connection I had lost with reality.[39]

Thus, it was suggested that the heroine, Selma, would escape from alienation by being part of the people. She would seek a way to serve her nation once again; consequently, she commits herself to teaching, as she did before to nursing during the years of the war of independence and before her move to Ankara.

Thus, women were expected to participate in social life and keep in step with the civilized world by undertaking "motherly" occupations such as teaching or nursing, and they should do so to serve their people and nation, but not for themselves or "their own small worlds." The position of women, as well as their proximity to or distance from civilization and the people, would be the determinants of the success of Kemalist reform. In other words, Kemalism looked for the synthesis between the project of civilization and the ideology of nationalism in the new image of women.

The new image of women as portrayed in the novels of Halide Edip Adıvar prepares the ground for the emergence of the Kemalist female identity. In her writings we encounter criticism of female characters who move away from national traditions by imitating the clothing habits, languages, and gestures of French women—welcoming their husbands in French, bargaining in French in Beyoğlu (the chic non-Muslim parts of the cosmopolitan Istanbul, also known as Pera), and asking their children to call them "mama."[40] She also, however, depicted women who were educated (in command of two or three foreign languages) and useful to their country due to their contribution to the labor force. These women, who left their femininity aside and who were identified with the goals of nationalism, were all "dignified, beneficial, hardworking members of society, companions, mothers of the whole nation such as the teachers and nurses of Yeni Turan, in contrast to those who were the decorative elements of their houses and sources of love to their husbands."[41]

As acknowledged by Berna Moran, Halide Edip Adivar created a new image of women in the synthesis between the two so-called conflicting value systems:

> In the eyes of the elite circle, sheltered, simple, and ignorant women, raised in accordance with the Islamic-Ottoman traditions as housewives, acted as the symbol of a backward civilization. Westernized, civilized women, on the other hand, lost their values, provoked suspicion among people because of their "free behavior" and were all uprooted. However, the heroines of Adıvar were successful in making a synthesis between the conflicting aspirations of women. For they concurrently remained loyal to their national values, and they were Westernized; they were educated and free, yet, at the same time, they were keen about their honor and modesty as women.[42]

The new image of Kemalist women was molded in such a context. Nevertheless, it can be acknowledged with confidence that the West-East synthesis of Halide Edip indeed leaned toward the East and Anatolian women. The significant difference between the populism of Halide Edip and the populism of Kemalism lies in their approaches to Islamic traditions. Halide Edip's conceptualization of populism does not embrace Islamic tradition. She established a relationship between religion and culture; religion was not confined to the world of worship and belief, and thus it was extended into the practices of daily life: clothing habits, fast breaking, presents given on holidays, children's games, and their entertainment, were all embedded elaborately into the world of customs.[43] Halide Edip was among the defenders of the *charshaf* (Islamic covering or veiling), which, for her, was the symbol of social integration, and she also assumed that wearing a *charshaf* would express nationalist feelings and the Islamic faith of the people.[44] The populism of Halide Edip, surrounded by Islamic tradition, can be deemed the mythical by-product of the national independence struggle.

In contrast with this, the Kemalist reforms directed toward the liberation of women from the oppression of religion encouraged not only the social but also the physical visibility of women. As found in the memoir of journalist and essayist Falih Rıfkı (1894–1971): "The reforms would rescue women. She had to be uncovered first, in order to be rescued. The harem had to be destroyed. Among the first actions came the removal of the curtains from the streetcars and boats of Istanbul."[45] Halide Edip in the meantime joined the "anti-Ankara camp" and objected to this decision as expressed in the following statement: "How do you interfere in our veils, in our curtains?"[46]

Regardless of the implementation of the established "national" and/or "religious" customs and traditions, the principle of civilization remained as the engine of social change. Leaving the years of the national independence struggle behind, the discourse of "integration with the people" was replaced by the will to educate the people on the path to civilization.

Kemalist Feminism: Public Visibility and the Egalitarian Social Imagination

The civilizing mission of the Kemalist project ceded "social visibility" to women. We can also reverse the argument: womens' attainment of visibility and their entrance into the public scene signified a change in civilization. The exit from the private sphere, the breakdown of segregation between the sexes, in short, the allocation of space for both sexes previously regulated by Islam, became subject to the impact of Western values. This impact, however, originated from the will of the state, embedded in Kemalist ideology and reforms.

The decrees of the Ottoman period, which regulated women's clothing as well as their appearance on the urban scene, were all reflected, in a sense, in the Kemalist reforms of the republican era.[47] In the Ottoman state, excursions by women in rowboats, visits to the "clotted-cream shops," promenading, the wearing of transparent mantles or outdoor veils and loose gowns (*yashmak*), had all been regulated by decrees since the sixteenth century. Women were required to behave in a decent manner, "to keep their veils in order to protect themselves against contact with strangers [*namahrem*]" and they were warned "not to walk out into the streets dressed inappropriately," particularly during Ramadan. Upon receipt of the information that "indecent behavior is occuring among men and women at the Bosphorus, Istanbul, and Üsküdar amusement resorts," the Ottoman authorities specified times at which women and men were allowed to go to the resorts separately.[48] A decree from the eighteenth century that forbade women from following fashion may be cited as another example:

> Some indecent women have started walking in the streets with strikingly arrayed clothes in order to corrupt people . . . and with bizarre head covers, imitating unbelieving women . . . All these strange clothes are forbidden. From now on women are not allowed to walk in the streets with those big-collared mantles, and they will not cover their heads with muslins bigger than three rounds . . . Otherwise, their collars will be cut off in public, and those who insist on such actions . . . will be exiled to the countryside.[49]

The visibility of women outside the *mahrem* sphere and the risk of exposure to the sight of men were perceived as the causes of the "intrigues" that violate the order of societies in which Islamic culture predominates. As set forth by Fatima Mernissi, in these societies the social order is guaranteed with the exercise of control upon female sexuality and women's isolation.[50] The Islamic social order measures its integrity by the honor of its women, which requires, in turn, the untouchability as well as invisibility of women. In Muslim societies political power and power relations between the sexes are interrelated. It is even more appropriate to suggest that the Islamic social organization is based on the limitation and prohibition of social encounters and promiscuity between sexes, rather than on the exclusion of women. In this context, Kemalist reforms aimed at subverting the social system based upon the segregation of sexes. There are many analyses that fundamentally claim that the Kemalist movement was limited to superficial superstructural changes independent of the economic structure, as is the case in Marxist analyses. Nevertheless, Kemalism is perhaps the first movement in the world that set the alteration of the existing civilization as its primary objective. It conveyed daily practices rather than political ones, collective identity and the definition of the relationship between the sexes, into the sphere of the Western cultural model. It targeted the everlasting point of differentiation between the Islamic East and the modern Western world—that is, the destruction of *mahrem*. Hence, Kemalists contended that the attainment of visibility for women and encounters between the sexes would bring about the conversion of civilization.

Consequently, coeducation of girls and boys starting from elementary school (with the exception of some European and American missionary schools), the professionalization of women, the granting of political rights to them, and the abandonment of veiling ensured the physical, urban, and public visibility of women, and all these reinforced the movement toward Westernist civilization in a Muslim society previously dependent upon the isolation of women. Muhaddere Taşçıoğlu described the transition from the veil, the symbol of segregation between the sexes, to the hat:

> The hat will not be used at once. The kerchief will be used for some time as the successor to the *charshaf*. The kerchief, which was initially tied under the chin, started to be used like the turban of today. Some women continued to cover their turbans with veils for some time. But they gradually left off the veil and the kerchief, and it was in the 1930s that the hat became much more widespread. This kind of kerchief lies in between the veil and the hat.[51]

It is clear that Kemalism encouraged physical changes (removal of the veil and *charshaf*), urban and public exposure (companionship of men and women in the same space), visibility of women, as well as the recognition of their citizenship rights (equal political rights). Beyond these it provided a legitimate, judicial base for these transformations. The new Civil Law is an example of this.

The Vector of Civilization: Civil Law

The principle of secularism, that is, the regulation of the relationship between men and women on the basis of a contemporary legal scheme rather than that of the Sharia, as well as the establishment of egalitarian relationships between the sexes, were all ensured by the new Civil Law with the advent of the Turkish Republic.

Kemalism remains a unique example among all political movements, for it is the only one that interfered with family law, the sphere most resistant to Westernization.[52] As noted previously, during the Ottoman period the focus of the controversies related to Westernization attempts was directed toward the religious regulation of the family institution. During the Tanzimat Period, however, a new regulation, based upon the principle of secularism, was introduced, yet this regulation was confined to contract, company, and commercial law. The regulation of personal status laws, including the law of family and of inheritance, however, remained under the domain of Islamic law.

In contrast to the process of Western modernity, which was molded by the changing affinity between state and church, modernization attempts in the Muslim countries derived their primary motive force from the revision of the existing civil law, as maintained by Niyasi Berkes.[53] Kemalism progressively came to prefer the Ottoman Westernists' views regarding the uniqueness and totality of civilization to the cultural originality of the Turkists. Discussions concerning the civil law seem to offer the best example for illuminating the Kemalists' preference for Westernism and civilization over the principle of nationalism. This noncompensatory attitude of Kemalists in favor of Westernist civilization is also visible in the legislation of the new civil law.

In 1923 a commission was established to prepare the new law.[54] The Turkist arguments of Ziya Gökalp dominated the commission, and it was therefore reasoned that the wholesale adaptation of any civil law from another country would be an inappropriate action. The Turkists argued that modernization would be actualized only if it was based upon the cultural customs and traditions of the country. The president of this commission and Minister of Justice Seyit Bey expressed his opinion on this issue clearly, as follows: "There exists a mutually shared principle of all jurists regardless of whether they are Westernists or Easternists that a nation is obliged to obey its customs and traditions. The laws of a nation are the products of its prevalent customs and they can only be altered along with the evolution of that nation's customs." Accordingly, the commission started to prepare a law based on the predominating traditions. The emergent bill was not exclusively loyal to the Sharia, while it consisted of some amendments to the existing law. In contrast to Ottoman civil law, the bill did not propose any segregation between Muslim and non-Muslim citizens, and, through this, it rejected the religious dogma that had been accepted as the backbone of the law.

Although the bill did not outlaw the practice of polygamy, it reminded the public that polygamy does not occur among the requirements of the Koran of Islam. Nevertheless, the bill did cite some of the "social" advantages of this institution. Polygamous marriages were claimed as important institutions in the prevention of prostitution, and, beyond this, they were regarded as a demographic solution to balance the distribution of sexes in the overall population, in which the female population exceeded the male, as a result of successive wars.

The bill fostered public discussions among Turkists, Westernists, and Islamists. While Islamists argued that the new law would wound the principles of Sharia, Turkists felt that the bill was inspired mainly by "religious ideology," instead of by positivism, and thus remained loyal to the Sharia. Westernists, however, were disappointed by the bill since their expectations were left unfulfilled. For them there could only be one existing civil law, as in the case of the civil law of the West.

It must be pointed out here that urban and educated women took part in all of these discussions, collectively. Answering the call of several women's associations and periodicals, a group of women gathered to discuss the bill on the law of the family in January 1924. Disapproving the "oppressive" attitudes of men, they discussed the need to establish new organizations in the defense of women's rights and founded a commission to examine the bill in detail. These meetings, which were closed to men, were severely criticized in the press. In opposition to the daily *Tevhit*, which argued that the women of Istanbul who "follow every tea party and indulge only in dancing and in fashion" cannot represent the "veiled Turkish rural women who undertook the whole responsibility of the country's prospect,"[55] Halide Edip defended these women, who, for her, seemed to be aware of the key effects of this law upon their future. Furthermore, in her response to the journalists who claimed that "all these women are making now is a useless rebellion against men,"[56] she defended their actions and the specific quality of their meetings. According to Halide Edip, women criticized certain articles of this bill concerning the institution of family with their own modes of expression; they set forth their criticisms not as jurists but as women who verbalized their own rebellion and sufferings, depending upon their own daily and personal experiences. In this passionate mode of women's expression, which targeted men's dominance, we might better see the signs of a rebellion that could trigger a radical social transformation, she wrote.[57] Thus, she became the spokeswoman of women's action in terms of both organization and collective goals.

The bill was taken under consideration once again two years later, in 1925, upon the order of Mustafa Kemal, when the minister of justice, Mahmut Esat Bey, graduate of the Faculty of Law in Switzerland, established a new committee composed of twenty-six jurists and university scholars. This commission was assigned to adapt Swiss civil law for application in Turkey. It is indeed the case that on 17 February 1926, the civil law, adapted from Swiss law with minor amendments, was forwarded to the National Assembly and was ratified in one session of Parliament without dissent. In opposition to those who insisted that the new law deepened the gap between the customs and traditions of the nation and the existing legal system, supporters of the civil law contended that the requirements of nations that are members of the civilized world are indistinguishable.

Examing existing affinity between the laws and the modernization process is worthwhile for understanding the Turkish case. Regardless of the fact that laws have functioned to institutionalize cultural change and social consensus in Western countries, their function in Turkey was limited to the determination and acceleration of the modernization process. While these laws served to mediate between the social actors in the West, they became the leading force of social change in Turkish society. The main objective of the civil law was not to "express" traditions and customs but, rather, to alter these traditions and customs along with the introduction of a new family structure running parallel to the requirements of modernity. To put it differently, the new civil law acted as the vector of nationalism. It is indeed a forceful vector, which pointed out the direction of change that traditions and customs, the regulators of relations between men and women, were expected to follow. What was at stake was whether or not it would be possible to put the civil law, defined by the Western principle of equality, into action in an Islamic country that was based upon the segregation and hierarchical relations of the sexes.[58]

The principle of equality, which maintains sovereignty over the social imagination of the West, lies beneath the ideal of progress. The history of the West is the history of continuous endeavors to revise its practice in light of the principle of equality. The equal rights of citizens (the French Revolution), equality between races (the abolition of slavery), equality between countries (anticolonialist movements), the equality of labor (labor-unionist and socialist movements), and, finally, the equality of the sexes (feminist movements) indicate the historical evolution of Western societies. The existence of the principle of equality within the social imagination of Western societies does not denote the existence of absolute equality in reality; rather, it directs the course of social change. Through the mediation of the equality principle Western societies define their collective identities and aim to transcend their individual selves. Muslim societies, however, are established upon the differentiation between men and women, and they embrace the patterns of hierarchical and vertical relationships between the sexes. The injection of the equality principle into the prevailing relations between the sexes via the implementation of the civil law in Turkey is indeed the reflection of the civilizational change upon the social imagination.

Kemalist Fathers and Their Modern Daughters

Fathers and their daughters were the agents of the egalitarian utopia during the Republican Period. The "silent agreement" maintained by progressivist fathers and their daughters, who were brought up on the Kemalist principles of civilization, determined the participation of women in public life.[59] Under the patronage of their fathers, and especially of Mustafa Kemat, symbolically the father of all Turks (Atatürk), the women of the republic undertook the assigned mission of fostering civilization through participation in social life.[60] To elaborate, participation in social life requires not only education, labor and the professionalization of women but also the visibility of women in urban settings. Süreyya Ağaoğlu, among the early female jurists of the Republican Period, described how everybody was shocked at a restaurant in Ankara, which was full of only male deputies, when she and her female friends (with the permission of their fathers) decided to have lunch out for the first time. She described how Atatürk then eased the situation by introducing them to the attendants at the restaurant.[61]

It is possible to argue that "Kemalist male psychology," which aspired to rearing female children under the guidance of republican principles,[62] did not lay down any barriers against the participation of women in social life; on the contrary, their involvement was encouraged. When the experiences of other countries, especially of the developed ones, are taken into consideration, it can be seen that sexist discrimination emerges as the most effective barrier against the attempts of women to coexist equally with men in the spheres of education, labor and politics. The Turkish case, however, diverges from all these experiences, for it was indeed the "support of men" (more significantly, the support of fathers and husbands) that enabled women to enter into public realms, as depicted in the case of female politicians in Turkey by Yeşim Arat.[63] Although the number of female deputies in Parliament has always been low, the maximum level being 4.5 percent, the political rights granted to Turkish women in 1934, prior to the granting of similar rights for French women, for instance, were among the sources of pride for Kemalists in their claims of progressivism and Westernism. The increasing visibility of women in the political realm directly reinforced the Kemalist Westernization efforts. The women of the early Republican Period were aware of their privileges, the result of the assigned mission of civilization, as stated clearly in the memoir of Hamide Topçuoğlu:

> We were really privileged; that is, in our small world we had the privilege of being "female student." All of the adults granted more appreciation to us and withheld it from the male students. We were the precursors of the republic, which aimed at the participation of women in public life and social relations with full responsibility and personal freedom.[64]

As much as the training of female students, the image of professionalized working women also defined Kemalist female identity. Permitting women to work was the main task according to Hamide Topçuoğlu: "We have interpreted professionalization in a different way: as if it was not for the purpose of earning a livelihood! It was much more important to serve, to be useful, and to be successful."[65]

"Kemalist fathers" and their "ideal daughters" thus injected the idea of equality between the sexes and the public visibility of women into the Turkish social imagination. Nevertheless, the socialization path followed by women, permitted by the will, approval, support, and regulation of men, was determined at the expense of the individual and sexual identities of women.

Freedom and Sexuality

Women's attainment of a new social identity outside the private realm became possible only when they stripped off their sexual identities. According to egalitarian liberal feminism, represented principally in the writings of Simone de Beauvoir, the liberation of women is equivalent to the freedom from captivity of femininity (the biology and nature of women). Emergence from the private familial sphere and their subsequent entry into the public arena would raise women to the level of humanity, free of femininity. Likewise, Kemalist feminism has defined the female identity by the principle that "a woman is a human being," and it supported the participation of women in the public sphere through their labor. Kemalist feminism found itself, however, in a position that obliged it to prove that women who gained visibility in public and worked with men were not deprived of their honor at all and, thus, did not pose any threat to public morality.

A caricature published in the daily *Akşam* in 1926 in reaction to the enactment of the civil law, depicts how the affinity between the freedom and honor of women is assumed to operate in reverse in society. The caricature depicts a woman who leaves "virtue, honor and shame" behind as an unnecessary load while she flies in a balloon.[66]

The entry of women into public life was legitimized only when the signs of her "esteem" were emphasized. Educated and professionalized women were among the glorified values of the Kemalist reforms, yet these women were "desexualized," or even masculinized, at the same time.[67] In other words, the Kemalist woman abandoned her veil and *charshaf*, yet it was at this time that she also "armored" herself and remained "untouchable" in public by veiling her sexuality.[68]

As is the case with the entrance of women into the public realm, which depended upon the extension of their motherhood roles, the relationship between men and women was defined in reference to the prohibitions that operate within kinship relations. The particular ways of addressing women, which are still often used today, including *bacım, hemşire, abla, ana,* and *yenge,* not only exerted prohibitions on the relations between the sexes but also lay down frontiers against the temptations of "interpersonal" and "anonymous" relations in the public sphere by assuming the existence of kinship relations. The cost of women's liberation may be witnessed in the repression of her "femininity," which is perceived as a threat to the existing social order, and even of her "individuality," in both urban and public realms (education, labor, and politics).

In her novel *Yeni Turan*, Halide Edip depicts the respectful ideal female character as someone "who rescued women from the state of being flesh and machine and who accompanied men as a virtuous, hardworking friend; a mother, governess of her children, and of her nation." Conforming with her assigned mission, she was not tempting at all: "There was no reminder of sex, neither masculinity nor feminity, in this look." She defined womanhood with the use of qualities like "sedateness" and "tenderness," which were ultimately associated with respect and motherhood.[69] It is the depiction of a female "teacher" in the novel that best symbolizes the image of Kemalist female identity. The teacher, on the one hand, loses her individuality and unselfishly legitimizes her profession in terms of her national mission and responsibilities, and, on the other hand, does not show any sign that would remind one of her sex. She is assumed to cling to the virtues of seriousness, sedateness, and modesty. In her uniform (two-piece costume, short hair, and light makeup) the teacher, though tender and educative (the extension of the motherhood role) as well as a leading social performer (soldier) in the Kemalist civilization mission, did not give credit to her individual "gender" identity as a woman.

Conversely, the novel by Adalet Ağaoğlu, *Ölmeye Yatmak* (Lie Down for Death) (published in 1973), exemplifies women in pursuit of their feminine identity and individuality. The entanglement of republican intellectual women with freedom and femininity is personified successfully in the leading character of the novel, Aysel, as pointed out by Hilmi Yavuz.[70] The ideological duality between traditional values, internalized within the familial context, and the Westernist republican ideology, encountered in the institution of education, is reflected in the consciousness of the female character as a conflicting situation between "being a woman" and "being an intellectual."[71] For her the only possible way to unchain herself from this duality lies in freedom—that is, intellectuality—by leaving her female identity behind. Nonetheless, this is not to be an enduring solution to her problem, for her repressed femininity reemerges either in her own desires or in the eyes of others. She finally engages in a relationship with one of her students, to whom she is superior intellectually, and discovers her femininity and becomes conscious of her own body: "I faltered in recognizing at once the very existence of this head, which was becoming a pile of ideas even when I was making love with my husband, this neck, these arms, these legs, this female body, which was forgotten for a long time in my own eyes." Nevertheless, the author did not liberate her female character, regardless of her discoveries of her own femininity, and at the end commits suicide over the fine distinction between "lying with a man" and "lying in death."[72]

From State Feminism to Individual Feminism

Stating that "state feminism" led to the emergence of a "schizophrenic identity" for women, Şirin Tekeli argues the idea that early republican women defined the boundaries of their lives within the framework of the national ideals and the zeal for duty assigned by the state, at the expense of their own personal wishes.[73] Hence, the Kemalist feminine identity, defined with direct reference to national ideals, started to be criticized from a feminist perspective.[74] Particularly since the beginning of the 1980s, an "autonomous" feminist movement has flourished in society. Giving credit to the fact that women entered the political realm along with their integration into the statist Kemalist, revolutionary leftist, and the traditional Islamic ideologies, Nükhet Sirman acknowledges that the women's movement will become more influential in society only when it is free of these movements and ideologies.[75]

Not only the detachment of feminism from Kemalist ideology but also its connections to leftist ideologies is questioned within the feminist movement. Feminist social scientists assert that the leftist ideology oppresses the gender identity of women as much as the Kemalist one does, pointing at feminism as an example of "bourgeois deviation" and a way of confining women to traditional roles.[76] As pointed out by Fatmagül Berktay, the leftist movement exerts control over the clothing habits and manners of women within the framework of revolutionary morality as a result of the assumption that women are much more prone to "becoming bourgeois" due to their nature. Regarding how the totality and integrity of the Islamic community is ensured through the regulation of women's morality, the leftist movement, too, defends itself against the "deviation" of women. The prevalent use of the cliché, bacı (the word often used by revolutionist men to address women; literally, it means "sister") suggests that leftist ideology welcomes women only as "female comrades," with their repressed sexuality and individuality, and, above all, this attitude designates its relationship with Islamic ideology, which regards women as the source of "intrigue" and excludes "personal erotic love."[77] The repressed femininity and individuality of women, whether in the name of Kemalism or the leftist ideologies—or, as we shall see, of Islamic ideology—are brought into question within the framework of power relationships between men and women.

In the last decade we began to witness the expression of women's sexuality and individualism, particularly in novels, magazines, and films. The films of Atıf Yılmaz, which focus primarily upon urban women, the magazine *Kadınca* (Womanly), and the books of Duygu Asena call for the discovery of women's individualism and sexuality beyond the roles of motherhood and wifehood, and they all aim at conveying the demand for equality between men and women, from the public sphere to the private realm and the inner worlds. Among all these the book *Kadının Adı Yok* (Woman Has No Name), by Duygu Asena, wholeheartedly defends the attempts of women to exert control over their own sexuality and desires, transgressing in a sense the taboo of women's "respectability," which basically relies upon the camouflaging of femininity, with the hope of revealing the repressed desires and gender identity of women. The individualism of women is on the agenda to the extent that women are speaking on their own behalf and not in the name of "other women."

The increasing number of observations regarding the "politicization of gender"[78] in political life—the feminist movement, the appearance of female ministers and female mayors, the quota assigned to women in the Social Democratic Populist Party—represent the entry of women as social actors into the public arena. As a consequence of the determination of a political agenda by the rising Islamist movements in the post-1980s, the question of women has once again entered the political sphere as the decisive criterion of societal choice between the dualities of East/West, progressist/reactionary, and secularism/Islam. Recalling the Tanzimat Period, the question of women has spurred political polarization. On the other hand, moving beyond a situation in which women were the objects of political struggle, they began to be the subject of politics. The feminist consciousness, established upon the exposition of the operating power relations between men and women, opens up a route for women to become social actors. Does the veiled Islamist women's movement, which occupied an important place in the political agenda of society during the last decade, pose a threat to these achievements by women? Do the rising Islamic movements aim at the reconstitution of a total Islamic system, principally based on the regulation of women and the homogeneity of social control, by establishing hierarchical and hegemonic relations that would displace the emerging social structure into which the liberal principle of equality has recently begun to penetrate? These questions remain to be answered.

CHAPTER 4

Veiling: The Symbol
of Islamization

Veiling as a political claim asserted by women, which has been witnessed throughout the Muslim world since the 1970s, questions the modernization experiences of the Muslim countries. The social and legal status of women define the stakes that the rising Islamic movements and the modernist elites confront. Furthermore, Islamization has gained visibility through the veiling of women; in other terms it is women who serve as the emblem of politicized Islam.

There is no doubt that the Iranian Revolution reinforced the existing identification between radical Islamism and the veiled women. Moreover, it was the female militants, with their black *chador* (Islamic covering), who imprinted the revolutionary uprising of the masses (mass mobilization) in the Western memory. The Islamic revolution has utilized the veiled bodies of women as a political symbol to show its difference from the Western world. In contrast to the French bourgeois or Marxist-socialist revolutions, which rested upon the principle of rationalism and criticism of exploitation, the Iranian Revolution introduced Islamic faith and identity into the political arena. The Iranian Revolution was depicted by the Western media as the "collective hysteria of the fanatic masses."[1] As a frequently used metaphor, the notion of hysteria was associated with feminine irrationality; the female body, with its "convulsions" and "hysteria," was equated with the chaotic order of the revolution.[2] The Islamic Revolution advanced the female body by giving it a new semantic language against Western civilization. Western culture locates the human body under the aesthetic and hygienic command of human willpower and the increasing submission of the human body to the spheres of science and secularization. The Muslim body, on the other hand, becomes a site for symbolic politics to the extent that Islamism attempts to politicize the distinctiveness of a religious conception of self and body. Thus, the image of veiled women serves to translate faith and religiosity into politics as a civilizational issue—that is, a distinct conception of self and body. Islamist movements display the interdependency between veiling and Sharia as well as between women and political power; they oppose the Western world not on the basis of a claim for a new political system but on that of the Islamization of the private and public spheres and the relationship with one's body and of the inner worlds. The public and political manifestation of the female body in black veils is the most meaningful and collective assertion of this Islamic conception of civilization. As such, the veiling of Iranian women has been the most visible symbol of a revolution; first, a voluntary symbol of a revolution unveiled by women; second a compulsory symbol of an institutionalized revolution.

Paradoxically, as Islam politicized itself, it moved women toward the political scene, and the black veil, the symbol of the return to premodern Islamic traditions, acted as an expression of the active participation of women in political demonstrations. Rising Islamist movements, on the one hand, call for the return of women to their traditional settings and positions. On the other hand, they replace the traditional portrait of a Muslim woman with a politicized, active one. The prevailing image of a fatalist, passive, docile, and obedient traditional Muslim woman was replaced by that of an active, demanding, and, even, militant Muslim woman who is no longer confined to her home.

This juxtapositon of the signs of traditionalism with those of militancy upset the Turkish public opinion, especially those groups that cherished modernist and secularist values. The emergence of post-1980 Islamist movements in the universities—and, more specifically, growing attention to the veiling issue in secular educational institutions, which are regarded symbolically as the "castles of modernity"—has concerned the public for the last ten years. The demands of female Islamist students for abolishing the ban on *turban* at the universities, expressed by sit-ins and hunger strikes in the larger provinces and at modern universities, not only annoyed and hurt the pride of Kemalist women but were also interpreted as intrusions on the secular, and Western, achievements of the country, that extend to the Reformist Period. The emancipation of women from religion and subsequent acquisition of the right to participate in fuller educational and social lives are clear benefits of secularism; nevertheless, the disappointments and political polarization caused by the demand for veiling— even though voiced by a limited number of women—have become significant social issues.

For the entire decade of the 1980s, the public in Turkey discussed the outlawing of the *turban*. It should be noted that this ban was sometimes violated in practice or, conversely, enforced severely; in 1991 it was finally abolished. While Islamists claimed that it is the right of every woman, according to the Koran, to wear a veil, the "progressive" group, consisting particularly of Kemalist women, argued that this demand jeopardized the principle of secularism: they then organized various associations, including Çağdaş Yaşamı Destekleme Derneği (Association of Support for Modern Life), Türk Kadın Hukukçular Derneği (Association of Turkish Female Jurists), and İstanbul Üniversitesi Kadın Sorunları Araştırma ve Uygulama Merkezi (University of Istanbul, the Center of Research and Application on the Woman Question). These Kemalist women's associations gave support to the principle of secularism wholeheartedly and systematically opposed the post-1980 Islamist movements. The political dualism between Sharia and secularism is expressed via the political confrontation that took place between the veiled and Kemalist women. Consequently, women, as social actors, have participated in political life and directed the public agenda, rather than being mere symbols of political conflicts.

It is in this context that the issue of the *turban* led to the polarization of secularists and Sharia supporters. Despite "liberal" claims, which emphasized that the state does not hold any right to intervene in the private life of individuals and that everybody is free to dress in the way he or she wishes and "tolerant" attitudes, which underlined the need to avoid exaggerating the question, arguments emerged during the discussion of the *turban* issue that the *turban* was more than a mere expression of individual choice, as part of the Sharia strategy to be followed by total covering (i.e., veiling and *charshaf*), hindered the flourishing of so-called liberal and tolerant attitudes.

Along with the discussions on the *turban* issue, the confrontation between fundamentalists and modernists during this period was exacerbated when Islamic students refused to have their pictures taken, "uncovered," for their university identification cards, when female medical school students refused to examine corpses, or refused to work with nude models in the schools of fine arts and, for example, even damaged sculptures and pictures. Furthermore, the issue became critical at the time of the National Holiday for Youth and Sports, when female students were asked to wear shorts in a symbolically significant public ceremony. While in the 1920s female students in sports festivals symbolized a change in conceptions of the self and the body—that is, the civilizational shift—in the 1980s veiled students stood for the rejection of this civilizational shift. In brief, shorts and the *turban* express Western and Islamic ideals, respectively, and once again the female body becomes a site for displaying societal preferences.

The affinity between the religion of Islam and the captivity of women was widely discussed in society once the Islamist movements gained strength. Consequently, the uncertainty about whether Kemalist benefits would be jeopardized through the subordination of women to men became widespread. Depending upon the Koran itself and its interpretations, the issues of polygamy, veiling, the required obedience of wives to husbands, the right of divorce given to men, and the right of men to beat their wives were often cited in discussions intended to prove that women are indeed enslaved by Islam rather than emancipated by it.[3] Various verses of the Koran depict women under Islam as physically weak and psychologically fragile, obedient to men by their very nature, and a means to satisfy men's lust; thus, the Koran did not grant equal rights with men and did not even regard women as individuals.

In conjunction with the analysis advocated on the basis of Islamic religion, the veiling movement is interpreted as a symbol of women's acceptance of obedience to men. The demand for veiling is characterized as part of the Islamist political strategy, as the tip of the iceberg; any sign of a role of women in this movement is simply explained with the assistance of conspiracy theories.

The politicization of the Islamic religion as an ideology, on the other hand, is generally explained by political scientists within the framework of the issues encountered in third world countries. According to these arguments, Westernist movements were originally inspired by "foreign ideologies," as witnessed in secularist Kemalism in Turkey and in the Arab socialism of Nasser in Egypt, and therefore, cannot take root in society. Thus, the problems encountered in Muslim third-world countries, such as economic recessions, hyperinflation, crumbling or nonexistent infrastructures in cities, alienated masses, and so on, brought about political instability and ideological discontinuity, and upon this the masses clung to the comfort of Islamic ideology, which stipulates "easy solutions" for social problems.[4] In other words, as a consequence of political repression, economic deprivation, and social alienation, it is asserted that Islam reinforces the national identity of the Muslim countries by setting them against the influences of Western countries.

Not only interpretations of the Koran but also political analyses that focused upon political and social connections in Muslim countries contributed to the apprehension expressed toward at the level of political ideology or toward the rules dictated by the religion itself. Nonetheless, social practice cannot be reduced to a "reaction" of the synthesis of economic and political factors, nor is there consistency necessarily between social practice and religious rules, or "the Book" itself. Otherwise, there would be no history. For history is written permanently on the basis of an articulation between the Book and social practice, between utopia and praxis. Books, rules, and political ideologies are interpreted differently, and they are transformed into practice in distinct ways by social actors. Hence, if analyses are confined to a framework of cause-and-effect, to the relationship between economic and political structures, the action of social actors cannot be comprehended fully. History is written from the tension between the subjectivity of social actors and the rules of social structures. Hence, I will incorporate the interpretation of the religion and of the movement itself from the eyes of the Islamist actors into my analysis, to better describe the meaning of the movement. The primary objective of this section, therefore, will be to analyze the significance of the symbolic system and the internal dynamics of the Islamist movement as well as the power relations between the political ideology and the gender system, rather than to investigate the "external" factors underlying the emergence of the Islamist movement on the basis of either a theological or a political explanation. This theoretical approach, which originates from the question of "meaning" rather than from a relationship of "causality," is in fact an extension of the hermeneutic tradition in social sciences. Thus, it is this hermeneutic approach, which aims to analyze the nature of social relations as well as the lifestyles rooted in a system of meanings, that is brought into this study, instead of "objective" science, which aims to determine universal laws.

Thus, the system of meaning embedded within the Islamist women's movement is analyzed by the method of sociological intervention, which gives priority to the agency and relationality of social actors. Needless to say, a quantitative study could easily and vividly portray the sociological profile of the issue—for instance, information on how many women veil themselves voluntarily or the educational and income levels of the parents of veiled students. Yet, this would fail to shed light on the political and social meanings of the movement. In addition, brochures, books, and other publications related to the Islamist movement could well be objects of a textual analysis. Although they provide us with information on the ideology of the movement, at the same time they fall short of explaining social dynamics underlying this social movement. The sociological method, however, which gives priority to agency, seeks to produce knowledge from in-depth and continuous interactions between social actors and the sociologist. The main objective of this approach is the interpretation, conceptualization, and theorization of the social practice, with an analytical distance, and this approach extends beyond one that mainly locates empirical information in the preferred theoretical models.

This study aims to uncover the nature of social relations and the embedded patterns of power detected in the analysis of a social movement. It, therefore, provides a route, and a new perspective, to move from a micro-level topic, (namely, the veiled women's movement), to macro-level issues affecting Turkish society, such as the conflictual interaction between Western civilization and Islam, modernity and religion, and the secularist elites and the fundamentalists. This research, it should be noted, has profited from the availability of quantitative data and prior analyses of texts. Since the main objective of the research is to depict the new social dynamics and the relations of power embedded within this movement, I will mainly focus on the interventionist sociological method.[5] In other words, the main goal of this study is to analyze the affinity between the political and gender power relations by placing this issue in the context of the relationship between modernism and Islam, moving away from the static description of the social condition of Muslim women. Let us now turn our attention to the way in which a new profile of Muslim women has moved onto the social platform by the veiled women's movement in Turkey, which constitutes the radical wing of the Islamist movement.

From Traditionalism to Radicalism

Although most veiled students come from Anatolian families, which practice Islam in its traditional forms, they differ significantly from their parents not only because of their higher educational level but, most important, because of the fact that they reject traditional interpretations of Islam. They embody the urban, educated, and militant new countenance of Islam.

The increasing strength of Islam in the society was influential especially on those who were born between 1964 and 1970. These young women started to veil themselves during their years of puberty and high school education, and they made their final choice to veil during their university educations. Most of these young women come from small Anatolian cities (although some of them are from Istanbul and Ankara), and their families have moderate levels of income.[6]

The conservative family background of these young women was a decisive factor in their orientation toward Islam. A senior at the School of Dentistry refers to her family and her experience of veiling in the second year of high school as follows:

> There is not one single reason [for veiling]. I was not living in a family unfamiliar with Islam anyway. It is my mother who first instructed me on religion. I mean, she was happy when I worshipped, and I also followed Koranic courses. My elderly relatives, people around me, were always encouraging. When I veiled they really loved, respected, me. By the way, my sisters are teachers, and they are all unveiled. However, I always thought that I would veil when I grew up, and I sometimes did. I gave my final decision when I was at the high school.

The lives of young women who come from families that practice traditional Islam but who have gone against the expectations of their families or relatives with their decisions to veil seem to follow a similar path. The case of a married woman from Fatih, a district in Istanbul, who was a junior at the Istanbul University School of Medicine recalls being repudiated by her close friends for her decision to veil:

I became familiar with Islam when I was a child. My grandmother and my father's female relatives were all veiled, and they were traditional people. But my father started to conduct the divine service, *namaz*, when he got his occupation. . . . and my mother started to veil after my birth. I was mostly raised by grandmother. I was brought up in Fatih. . . . I was about eight or nine years old when my grandmother sent me for Koran courses around Ulucami. You know, children are always registered to Koran courses during their summer holidays—that's it. That was really it at that time. In my family, among my close relatives, there is no veiled person. . . . I was really regarded as an odd person when I veiled and put on my long overcoat. They asked me to unveil, and they were really insistent. They were hard on me. Each time I came home, they tried forcefully to unveil me; they were asking me how I could do this to them and why I am like this. . . . My sister is still unveiled, for example.

As shown in these passages, although these young women were reared in traditional religious families, their decision to veil was regarded as an "exaggerated" act, and this decision caused problems between the young women and their families. The families objected to the veiling particularly because they feared that their daughters would not be able to pursue their educations anymore, that they would be isolated from society, and that they would not be able to have a happy married life.[7] Furthermore, as illustrated, many of the young women's own sisters are not veiled. A female Islamic student at the School of Dentistry whose sister is a teacher expresses her experience with her mother and sister as follows:

> At the very beginning, my mother was angry at my decision to veil. And when I put on the overcoat she accused me of passing beyond the limits. She warned me seriously not to dress like that. My sister is a teacher, so she doesn't veil. She cares what she wears, and she sews herself. And I had long discussions with her when I veiled, since she doesn't approve of my dress.

The young women in large cities started to veil during their university educations, regardless of whether or not they came from conservative families. A student from Eskişehir, for example, a graduate of a religious high school (İmam Hatip) who studied psychology at the University of Istanbul, explains that nontraditional veiling styles (wearing turbans and long overcoats) are a phenomenon of metropolitan cities:

> I was attending İmam Hatip during my secondary school years, and I was covering my head there and left it uncovered in the house regardless of whether there was a man in the house. . . . But I could not cover up when I was in Eskişehir. I came to Istanbul for my high school degree. When I attended the university I could cover my head and put up a long overcoat, as I wished.

For these young women, who generally came from traditional families and small provinces, the act of veiling is on the whole an urban phenomenon and also related to their experiences in the education process. Veiling by young women cannot easily be explained either by its enforcement by male members of the family, the impact of rural traditionalism, or the effects of religious education. The young women, who mostly had secular high school education, cover themselves by their own wills, and, in addition, their interpretation of Islam contradicts the traditional understanding of Islam that their parents maintain. The more they have encountered the radical and political interpretations of Islam, the more they have gone through a process of differentiation, which has sometimes resulted in conflicts with their close relatives. They have increasingly distanced themselves from their parents and traditional Muslim people in every possible way. Although, in their own words, "they had so many things in common with the people," they indeed refer to the holy books as "sources" and hold "inquiries" on them, in contrast to "traditional believers," who uncritically accept religious obligations. Criticizing inherited traditional Islam, embedded in enduring customs and traditions, they commit themselves to the religious knowledge of Islam by turning to the sources. Unlike the "ignorant" masses, who experience traditional Islam on the basis of "hearsay," they perceive themselves as "enlightened" and "intellectual" people. Although it seems that they are fairly close to the traditional people around them, they stress their difference from these people:

> Those people do not have anything, except hearsay and traditional Islamic information. Their information definitely does not rely on inquiry. Would you believe that there is a deep gap between my parents, my grandmother, and me? You would probably think that we are so similar to each other, thanks to this scarf and this long overcoat, wouldn't you? . . . But their Islam is just hearsay. They tell us with surprise that we invent new rules in Islam.

The differences among various styles of veiling represents the distinction between the traditional people and these Islamic young women. From the young women's standpoint, traditional people who cover their heads, but who, at the same time, leave their hair and necks uncovered, do not practice true veiling because they are ignorant about Islam:

> First of all, women do not know what veiling really means. The main purpose of veiling is to hide beauty. We see around us those who cover themselves traditionally, leaving their necks uncovered. You know, you should not leave your neck uncovered. Their hair is visible; their shirts are short-sleeved.

Coming from traditional backgrounds, these young girls criticize the traditional practices of Islam as well as the "current understanding of religion." "This is why these young women, who were familiar with the Koran and Koranic concepts in a different vein, who were in command of sociology and historical perspective of Islam, and who claimed the integrity of politics and religion, looked odd to their parents, who considered religion solely as a matter of worship and a pure conscience."[8] Compared to their parents, these youngsters stand in a different and more prestigious position due to their knowledge of Islam (they are familiar with a different interpretation of the Koran) and also their university educations (they are in command of history and sociology). These are the main factors that make the girls "literatate" and, even, "intellectual." They hold a stronger voice in public as long as they extend the limits of religion from personal worship and the question of conscience to a collective political movement. The politicization of religion encouraged faith to appear on the scene as an alternative vision, in opposition to Western civilization, and prepared the ground for the emergence of a "radical Islamist movement." In returning to the sources and leaving traditions behind, the Islamist movement, as a political force, suggests the transformation of society and of the world as an alternative lifestyle to that of the West.

In this radical Islamist movement, focused on the criticism of traditions and Western modernism, Islamist women play a significant role. The veiling of educated and urban Muslim women speaks for radical Islam. Hence, the use of *turban* instead of head scarf (*başörtüsü*) and the semantic difference between the two designate the new profile of Muslim women. As distinct from the widespread use of the scarf, which is a reminder of traditional customs and habits in country provinces and urban ghettos, turbans draw the attention of people as a reminder of the threat of "fundamentalist movements" when the political and collective power of religion is used against traditionalism. Above all, it moves Islam from the "periphery" to the "center." The phenomenon of Islam, on the one hand, geographically moved into urban settlements and, on the other, penetrated the central power apparatus where modern cultural values and symbols are created.[9] Veiled women are not simply passive conveyors of the provincial traditional culture; they are, rather, active and self-asserting women who seek opportunities in modernism. They have come into the public scene not at the periphery, where traditions prevail, but in the urban settlements and the universities, where modernism flourishes. In this context veiling symbolizes radical Islamism, which is molded on the tension between traditionalism and modernism.

The Veiled Sexuality

According to Islam, the prescriptions regarding veiling by women represent the social order of the Islamic community, which is based on the bipolarity of the sexes. The segregation of the sexes is demarcated naturally at the level of clothing. Clothing fulfills a moral function in Islam, the preservation of the honor of women. Clothing as the instrument of morality must not expose the anatomical features of the female body but, rather, should hide them. The books of law, *fıkıh*, lay down in detail the way clothes must be worn. The clothing rules of Islam, principally established upon the segregation and differentiation of the sexes, rest on the reinforcement of the symbols of femininity and masculinity. While veiling represents hidden femininity, the beard represents a man's masculinity.[10]

Veiled women themselves have internalized the need to regulate one's sexuality. Their answers to the question of why they veil point to the relationship between veiling and sexuality. A woman's honor is strictly dependent on her veiling: "A Muslim woman who prefers veiling is in fact the defender of her honour."

By veiling herself, a woman exercises control over her behavior and limits her appeal; thus, she maintains her purity: "The veil is not just a concrete thing, a piece of cloth. It is indeed the attempt to reduce the attractions of any woman to the lowest possible degree in her behavior, conversation, and in ways of sitting and standing." If feminine attributes are revealed, men will be tempted; hence, women are obliged to protect themselves from being looked at: "It is necessary to veil so as not to become the object of men's gaze." The sexuality and even the beauty of women represent threats to the social order: "Beauty must be kept hidden in order not to cause disorder and intrigue."

Thus, the veiling of women maintains the boundaries between the sexes as well as preserving order in the community. Islamist women in covering themselves hide their sexuality by their own will. It is even the case that the regulation of female sexuality, expressed in the idea of hiding and concealing oneself from the sight of men, may turn into an "obsession." Despite the fact that she stood alone in the group discussion, a psychology student expressed her obsession with concealment by her preference for *charshaf* (black Islamic covering): "I do not consider scarves and long overcoats as veiling at all. I sometimes looked at someone twice or three times when I was walking in the street. This is why I support the idea of complete veiling; *charshaf*, dark glasses, and gloves."

Fatima Mernissi, in her book, *The Political Harem*, defines three distinct functions and dimensions of the concept of veiling. The first dimension is visual, and its function is to conceal "oneself from the look." The second dimension is related to space; its purpose is to set boundaries between the sexes and, thus, separate them. The third dimension, however, refers to a moral principle concerning "the forbidden act": veiling points out the forbidden sphere.[11]

As Mernissi maintains, the veil, or "curtain," was initially intended to draw a boundary between two men rather than between women and men. Mernissi further argues that the verse of the Koran on veiling in fact emerged in response to an event in the community in which all values had been lost. She explains this event with reference to the interpretation of Tabari: the Prophet got married and desired to be left alone with his new wife, Zeyneb, but he failed to get rid of a group of men who were lost in discussion. The veil was the response of Allah to this society, which lacked proper manners and which hurt the timid Prophet, who had hesitated to explain the situation to his guests.[12]

In other words, for Mernissi, veiling initially aimed at preserving personal intimacy and privacy between men and women. The Koranic verse about veiling was set forth by the Prophet to divide the Muslim community into two distinct worlds: the inner world (the home) and the outer world (the public sphere). But, over the course of time, veiling began to symbolize "sexual discrimination" and the "confinement of women."[13]

Therefore, since it hides women from the gaze of men and determines the boundaries between the sexes, the veil signifies the *mahrem* sphere on the basis of strict religious recommendations. This arises from the fact that the unity of the community is strongly dependent on the honor of men (*şeref*), which is estimated in relation to the purity of women, as maintained in the private sphere.

As distinct from Western societies, private life in Muslim societies is directly associated with the sexuality of women and the forbidden zone (*mahrem*) itself. *Mahrem* means "intimacy," "privacy," "secrecy," and "silence." But, at the same time, it is another word for "unlawful" (*haram*)— that is, canonically prohibited acts and relations as well as "concealment from the look of a male stranger."[14] In other words, the Islamic order of society is established not only on the regulation of inner and outer spaces but also on the privacy of women. The act of veiling refers to the *mahrem* sphere. In conforming to this cultural standard, Islamist women underline their difference from Western civilization and uphold the hiddenness of female sexuality. As one student mentioned:

> People in the West manifest their sexuality in an enlarged dimension through embellishing themselves, but this in fact impoverishes sexuality. We do the opposite of what they do at all possible levels, and we confine sexuality to certain spheres as much as we can. That is, we try to take sexuality away from attention in the outside life, the streets, and in the public realm."

The magazine *Mektup*, which favors complete covering with the use of a *charshaf*, veil, and gloves, explains its attitude toward veiling as follows:

> We can never go into the streets with our house dresses; if we do so, we will expose ourselves to lustful gazes and will become a source of disorder for the Muslim community. . . . To increase our attraction to our husbands inside the house and to decrease it outside are our fundamental principles. That is to say, we will be appealing in the house and repulsive outside.[15]

Calling for women to be "pretty in the house and ugly outside," this magazine radically defines the concept of civilization as distinctive from the West in an active, demanding, and militant fashion.[16]

Difference from the West is among the primary concerns of Islamist movements in contemporary societies. This is why the Islamic order, which "wants to see Muslim people not as imitators of other people but as honorable in themselves," assigns importance to veiling.[17] As witnessed in the Iranian revolution, too, when the concern over differentiation and opposition between the West and the East was intensified, veiling symbolized both rejection of the Western cultural model and the expression of the Islamic identity. Again, politics and sexuality became intertwined in an encounter between the West and East.

The Educated Muslims

Veiling as a political statement is mostly witnessed among female university students. The standard arguments for the rise of Islamic movements that focus on "ignorant" and "unemployed" social groups from rural areas, still influenced by traditional values and isolated from modern society—since they have not yet become educated or realized the opportunities for money making in urban settlements—fall short of explaining the real situation. Nevertheless, Islam, which had been identified with rural traditions and ignorance, started to undergo a process of change since Kemalist modernization. As is the case in many other Muslim countries, the Islamist movement in Turkey has begun to influence doctors, pharmacists, engineers, lawyers, psychologists, in short, the professionals of the future.[18] The contemporary actors of Islamism are university students, future intellectuals, and professionals, not marginal, uneducated, frustrated groups. Consequently, these people, who will be in control of prestigious positions in society in the near future, do not stand outside society but, rather, "are certainly inside it."[19]

The participants in the group discussions who were senior or junior students at the Medical School of Cerrahpaşa, the School of Dentistry, and the School of Pharmacy Marmara University, the Department of Philosophy at the University of Istanbul, and others, are examples of success in education. They express the importance of education on every possible occasion. Admission to the School of Medicine is equated with idealism:

> My primary goal was to register in the School of Medicine. I really wanted this, and I did. I was very eager for the school. So are all students of the Medical School, in fact. But, with the onset of the turban prohibition, I lost my enthusiasm and felt aversion to the school . . . I was sadly thinking of what I could do at home. Up to this year, this is my third year in the school, I never failed a course and, when I failed this year because of absence, it was really difficult for both my parents and me. I do hope that next year there will not be any more problems. Because I really want to pursue my education in medicine.

The veiled students pointed out in the group discussions that women must educate themselves as a requirement of the Islamic religion, despite the widespread baseless claims that Islam acts as a barrier against women's learning. A student from the School of Dentistry criticized the derogatory image of Muslim women: "They claim that Islam forbids education to women. This is a totally false image. Muslim women, too, can have access to science, and, in fact, this is a requirement." Another student, in philosophy, complained about the identification of Islam with ignorance: "There is a widespread belief in society; it is the housewives who cover themselves, and, if you study and graduate from the university, then you will not cover yourself."

The pursuit of education and success in university entrance exams are appreciated by these students' families. For the families, who invest their futures in the education of their children and who sacrifice everything for this achievement, the enrollment of their daughters in the university is among their sources of pride. Thus, they cannot understand why their daughters would jeopardize their achievements in education by their decision to veil. On top of this, despite the education they have received, their daughters appear unwilling to enter into the modern urban world their parents dreamed of for them. They seem to be tangled in a tug-of-war between education and an inclination toward Islam. As one student explained: "They were no longer in a position to be proud of saying 'Our daughter attends the university.' People who have seen me assumed that I am, rather, enrolled in a Koran course."[20]

The phenomenon of modernization is generally assumed to follow a unilateral path of evolution different from that of traditional attachments and religious belief systems, toward the transition to modern society.[21] Education and urbanity, which are considered to be prerequisites to modernization, are regarded as clashing with the practice of veiling, which expresses commitment to Islam. The veiling of an educated woman suggests a paradoxical situation. As we have seen in the Turkish case, the definition of a "civilized" person is identified with a certain way of life, the product of modernization. Thus, an educated person is an "intellectual," "enlightened" one, freeing him or herself from the conservatism of the Islamic religion and traditions. In opposition to Islamic traditionalism, the definition of progress derives its basic characteristics from a civilized way of life and education. The prevalent dualities between progressivist/reactionary and educated/ignorant also play a part in the conflict between intellectuals and Muslims. Islamist female students who, on the one hand, acquire the label "educated," and who, on the other hand, are committed to Islam, subvert these preestablished categories. Thus, Islam represents the dark side of the history of Turkish modernization experiences, and it contributes to the formation of a new identity for newly emerging educated social groups. The profile of educated veiled Muslims not only challenges the shift of civilization but also the power domain of Westernist elites.

Abdurrahman Dilipak, one of the leading figures of the Islamist-backed Welfare Party and an Islamist intellectual, drew attention during an in-depth interview to the birth of a new Muslim profile, criticizing the labeling of Islamists as conservative people in a sarcastic manner:

> Why should we be the reactionaries? We have not ruled this country for the last sixty years; we do not have money, nor have we weapons. And the label they stigmatized us with does not match the reality today. The Westernist elites are distressed by educated Muslim women, who are in command of foreign languages as well. You can no longer identify Muslim people with either illiteracy or backwardness. We Muslim people do not fit the everyday definitions of reactionary people anymore.

The emergence of a new profile for Muslim women gave rise to public annoyance, and Islamic students believe the reason they were frustrated in their educational activities was related to this emergent profile. A student at the School of Pharmacy touched upon this:

> They are angry at us, because we are successful in our courses. They label us "veiled heads." How can we be good at our courses unless we can concentrate on them? They cannot accept us, and this is precisely why they set many barriers in front of us, and this is why they oppress us.

The more these women enter the urban spheres and educational institutions, the more they become part of the Islamist movement in the name of defending their Islamic identities, in contrast to others' expectations. They turn toward modern institutions yet retain the expression of their politicoreligious identities. They uncover their Islamic identities in the universities, urban places, and the political arena, and this enables them to mold their new profile of the Muslim woman. The increasing visibility of the image of the educated, militant-Muslim woman in places occupied by Westernist elites signifies a challenge to the old elites as much as it signifies the opposition between the West and Islam.

The Desired but Forbidden Public Sphere

How do Islamic women, who pursue university educations, who remain loyal to Islamic principles, and who cannot give up either their turbans or university degrees, legitimatize their entry into the public sphere? In other words, how, in their narratives, do they interpret their entrance into the public sphere and, particularly, their encounters with men? How do they juxtapose their religious beliefs, involvement in collective movements, and professional expectations? How is it possible that Islam, the confiner of women to the private sphere and regulator of social life on the basis of the separation of men and women, becomes the politicoreligious ideal of these education-oriented women?

The idea that Islam does not set a barrier against the education of women had already been accepted in group discussions. Nevertheless, the question of women working following their education was still problematic. The first response to this question came from a female writer for *Kadın ve Aile* (Women and Family) magazine, who objected to women working:

> I do not agree with the idea that women should work. Because, according to our beliefs, the principle role of women is to raise children, that is, motherhood. . . . There is no obligation to work. But in our religion it is obligatory to learn science. I mean, both men and women must master science. Therefore, they study to learn something; we need this much at least for the children we are going to raise.

The other participants also supported this view and assigned primary importance to the domestic tasks of women. Education does not seem to be a goal per se; for them the happiness of the family and the training of children are women's primary responsibilities: "It is really the case that working is not a goal in itself. The main issue here is the family, that is, to run it properly and to train children accurately."

Despite the fact that they recognize the right to education for women, the attitudes of Islamist magazines, which limit the opportunities of women by confining them to rather narrow worlds, follow the same direction and thus place the motherhood and wifehood roles of women before the ideal of working outside the house.[22]

Nevertheless, the discussions opened up new paths regarding the possible working conditions that would not conflict with women's motherhood tasks:

> The regulation of working hours is what really matters. This is why I have chosen to specialize in dentistry. You can set your own working hours at your office. Or you can have your clinic at home. Besides this,

> I thought that I could serve women in this profession. Any close rela-
> tionship of a woman with a man, even if he is a doctor, is not tolerated,
> although it is permissible in our religion. If I have a clinic in the future,
> I will work there for my family. My family will be above everything.

As can be seen from this passage, women are timidly trying to legitimize
their desire to work in their fields of specialization with reference to Islam,
and they give assurances that they will not leave aside their primary roles
as defined by Islam. Regardless of how much importance is attached to
education, once it comes to working, they claim that no causal relationship
exists between education and working.

In the course of discussion, the sociologist intervened so as to scruti-
nize the role conflict the participants were experiencing between loyalty to
the traditional Islamic female identity and the professional identity they
had acquired during their education. The sociologist questioned their
degree of determination in pursuing an education, reminded them of the
costs they were paying, as they claimed, in return for their persistence in
finishing their education, and raised the issue of working:

> You told me that you have joined in demonstrations and struggled to
> defend your right of education at the universities you were eager to
> attend. And, once again as you told me, in response to the outlawing
> of the turban, you decided to wait and continue your education after
> the removal of this ban. So, what I want to ask is how do you explain
> your commitment toward education solely by reference to your moth-
> erhood tasks? Isn't professionalization one goal of education? Are all
> of your efforts for the constitution of a family?

The Islamist women attempted to solve their inner conflict between loyalty
to Islam and the desire to work by referring to the cost that Western working women pay. In addition, criticizing the efforts of Western women who
want to prove their self-sufficiency by working, they underline their difference from them:

> You have in mind the question of economic independence and self-
> sufficiency. None of our friends here aim to prove anything. We want
> to be useful; we want to serve Muslim women. This is the reason why
> we don't have any ambition to be the best. You cannot compare this to

the West. For Western women, this appears as the attempt to prove their own identity.

Disapproving of the individualism Western women acquire by working, the students regard their aspirations to work as an integral part of the collective Islamist movement and orient this toward the benefits of society. The question of working, for women, which symbolizes the degeneracy of Western society, reinforces the ideological armor of Islam. They oppose the liberation of women by working, and they support the idea of the modesty of women as depicted in Islam. The participants of the group discussion compared the position of women in Western and Islamic societies to show that the superiority of Muslim women originates from their status in the family.

It was argued in the group discussions that Western women were not liberated but exploited when they began to work:

An industrial revolution occurred in Europe. Women started to work in factories as a consequence of this industrial revolution. They were forced to work there as second-class workers with half the payment men received. Then women started to struggle everywhere against the fact that they were treated as second-class citizens. After all this, we have started to witness their attempts to show their self-sufficiency.

It was also argued that the equality between men and women was fictitious, for women continued to assume household tasks at home along with their labor outside the home; thus, their responsibilities were in fact doubled. The image of Western women has changed also from the standpoint of these "educated" Muslim women. Western women are no longer depicted according to moral terms such as *permissive, loose,* and *degenerate* by these women; rather, they now question the social achievements of Western women.

Cihan Aktaş, one of the outstanding female Islamist intellectuals, analyzes the question of working women with reference to capitalism. She suggests that for women to "work outside" generally means the exploitation of their labor or the abuse of female sexuality. To cite from her study: "their existence. . . . [is] as either a cheap labor force in the capitalist workplace or an insatiable consumer group targeted by this system."[23] Although women work "outside," they are still kept away from productive, creative jobs. For Aktaş the reason why Islamist students have reservations about working life stems from "the offensive dimensions against women embedded in a capitalist working life."[24] Working life is criticized, since it can be equated with the daily nine-to-five working hours, traffic jams, low payment, sexual harassment, and alienation of the individual. It is interesting to note that the question of women and working life is taken into consideration not with reference to the Koranic verses but to the prevailing social structure. A Muslim intellectual analyzes the question of working women with the assistance of categories such as "cheap labor exploitation" and "producer-consumer," which recall the vocabulary of the Marxist tradition. The Marxist and feminist critiques of Western intellectuals, which are directed at the progressivism and modernism of industrial society, seem to influence the theoretical frameworks of Islamist intellectuals.

Although Islamist women criticize the social position of Western women from a historical perspective using Western paradigms, they idealize the social position that Muslim women assume. A senior student at the School of Arts idealized Islam to the extent that she even defended the "child-woman" position of Muslim women:

> According to our religion, a woman is the lady of the house. Men are obliged to take care of them [the women]. They are asked to fulfill their needs. This is totally placed on the shoulders of men. Men respect them highly. But let us now look at the working life and the conditions of men in the West. Following the entrance of women in the working life, they are really worn out, both physically and spiritually. They want to prove that they are self-sufficient, but they are worn out in this attempt. They work both at home and outside. Their husbands, however, work only outside. I don't know, I heard that there are some men who wash dishes, but I can't imagine. . . . Personally, I don't think I will work. What I am saying is that the real place where women belong is in their homes; that is, I belong in my home. Working brings division and weakness to the family. Well, we are young, education is obligatory, and we have to study. But later we are supposed to serve our families, and we should bring up our children according to what we have learned.

The issue is closed with a clichéd attitude: "In Islam women already assume a high status, and thus they do not have to struggle for liberation."

The discussion, which underscored the traditional domestic tasks of women, in the end moved beyond this reinforcement and found the legitimate ground of women's education in the "service to Islam." What is interesting here is that it is the men who remind women of the "real" reason why they pursue education. The sudden intervention of the one and only male employee of an Islamist magazine for women changed the course of the discussion by pointing out the personal desire of women for their professions, exalting their collective and political identities within the Islamist movement:

> I suppose another influential factor why my friends attend schools is to realize the transmission of Islamic knowledge to other people, that is, to use Islamic terminology, *tebliğ* [transmission of Islamic faith] rather than to work anywhere . . . There are prestigious professions in society, such as doctors and pharmacists. In case one of our veiled friends holds a position as a doctor or a pharmacist, she may assume that she will probably serve *tebliğ* much more easily.

The group welcomed this comment, offered on behalf of women, and stressed service to Islam as the primary objective of their educational pursuits: "For us, education, the diploma, is definitely not a goal. It is only a means toward our ideal, which is transmission of Islamic faith."

Although the members of the group discussion were strongly motivated for education, they found themselves at pains to express a willingness to work. Their difficulties came from, on the one hand, the Islamic male-oriented ideology, which permits education for women only for the transmission of Islam, and, on the other, the religious rules that confine women to the private realm and assign only the roles of motherhood and wifehood.

The conflict between loyalty to Islam and the desire for their occupations turned either to criticism of Western modernism or of traditionalism. Returning to the sources of Islam, they idealized the Golden Age of Islam and tried to prove that their new lives did not contradict the essence of Islam. The entry into social life, companionship between women and men, and the active and militant image of women in contrast to the sacrificing maternal image, were all affecting their practices. But how compatible was their public visibility and mixing with men with the rules of Islam? It was the Golden Age of the first four caliphs that provided the ideal model of society that could solve the conflict experienced by female Islamic students. Returning to the Golden Age of Islam, they not only would abandon the burdens of traditional Islam but also would be able to seek alternatives to Western modernism.

Islamic Utopia

The designation of the difference between the customary practice of Islam and the Islamist way of life during the Golden Age opens up a route for radical Islam to distance itself from traditionalism. Paradoxically, fundamentalism—that is, returning to the origins of Islam—permits a critique of customary Islam and a way to cope with modernity. The return to the past enables Islamist women to reconcile their social-professional demands with their Islamic identities. In a manner similar to the ideologues of the radical Islamist movement, they seek the answers for the current questions of the modern world in the period of the Golden Age of Islam. In other words, the myth of the foundational period of Islam provides a utopia for Islamist movements trying to come to terms with Western modernism.

The Islamist students argue that equality between women and men in fact existed in the Golden Age of Islam, and the unequal division of sex roles and the oppression of women result from the misinterpretations and mispractices of Islam. It is claimed that Islam, in its "essence," recognizes full rights for both men and women intrinsically; women hold the right to education, and domestic tasks are assigned to men as well as women. Islamist students argue that the idea of equality between the sexes is not at all unfamiliar to Islam. As one student stated:

> Let me give an example from my own family. I sometimes talk about the verses and hadiths of our Prophet to my father. "Father, when it was necessary, our Prophet undertook his own tasks and helped his wife; he swept the house." . . . "Where, " he asks, "where is it written?" That is, they don't know such things, and they don't accept them. Since they have not heard it from their own parents, they don't believe in such things in Islam. They have been shown just that the women in the West struggle for equality. In Islam it is impossible for women to be equal with men. For them women are respected so much in Islam, why should they ask for equality?"

The definition of women in relation to domestic tasks is not a religious requirement, and women are even involved in trade, as described in the course of the group discussion:

Cooking, dealing with domestic tasks, and others are not religious obligations in Islam. That is, in Islam there is no such thing as you will do these, your husband will earn money and maintain the family. Women give all these as alms. If a woman undertakes these, it is just as a favor. This is such a favor that men should thank them in return. In case men are wealthy enough, women always have the right to ask for a maid; they can even ask for a wet nurse for the child . . . On the other hand, according to Islam, women are always allowed to trade with their own goods and capitals; men cannot interfere with this. Women can spend their profits for their own needs and wishes.

The arguments that support the claims that inequality between men and women is embedded within society and does not originate in Islam itself are defended by respected Islamic intellectuals, and the Koran is interpreted in this vein. For instance, in his book *Kadının Çıkış Yolu* (The Way out for Women) Hüseyin Hatemi states that the equality between men and women is "the fundamental principle of the Koran" from the standpoint of human rights, countering the accusations of "Westernism." He attempts to prove, with the assistance of the Koranic verses, that Islam does not regard women as second-class human beings. Taking the most ambiguous rules into consideration, such as "man is the head of the household," "veiling of women," "the right given to husbands to beat their wives," "polygamy," "the right of divorce recognized for husbands," and others, he argues that these rules are either misinterpreted or originate from "concocted hadiths" and in the end become "established prejudices." Hatemi further maintains that the distinct position occupied by men in Islamic jurisprudence springs from the natural difference between the two sexes, which assigns certain tasks and responsibilities to men, and it must be recognized as *"primus inter pares"* (the first among the equals). He asserts that equality between men and women in Islam is "absolute" not only at the abstract level, from a philosophical point of view, but also in the profane sphere of human rights:

As it is the case with the impossibility of establishing various discriminations among human beings on the basis of race, colour and ancestors, from the angle of human rights it is not possible to set discrimination between men and women on the basis of sex, either. Allah did not create women for men; they are created for each other. Women in this world need the clothes of men, so do men need women's clothes.

To conclude, Hatemi elaborates on the conservative thesis that fuels the principle of difference yet, at the same time, of the complementarity of the sexes.[25]

There are other sources that pay attention to the difference between the Koran and the conventional customs and habits. In an ethnological study of Mediterranean countries Germaine Tillion disclosed that oppression and colonization of women do not originate in Islam, but, rather, are a cultural phenemenon observed in both Christian and Muslim countries. Tillion argued for the specific structure of family as the source of women's oppression. It is even claimed that the rights recognized for women by the Koran exceed the traditions of societies during the era in which the Koran was revealed.[26] Comparing Christian and Muslim women in Mediterranean countries, Tillion argues that in Christian countries Catholicism remained fundamentally an "archaic and masculinist" religion, whereas in Muslim societies the customs and habits remained backward, despite the "Koranic revolution."[27] To paraphrase Tillion, if Mediterranean women are subdued, this occurs against the will of the Koran: prevailing customs and norms are what monitor sexuality and reproduce community and family life, which are the causes underlying the "imprisonment of women."

The well-known Moroccan sociologist Fatima Mernissi, too, elaborates on this cultural heritage that hinders equality of the sexes. She seeks the basis for equality between the sexes in the question of whether it is necessary to "abandon" the Arabo-Muslim past completely or is it more reasonable to accept this past, but to subject it to a process of "selection." Following the latter path, she returns to early Islam and recalls that the main objective of the Prophet was to set up a democratic as well as a religious community in which both women and men would discuss together the laws of Medina and would participate equally in the foundation of a strong and monotheistic state in Arabia. Citing the well-known female figures of Medina, including Um Selma, Sakina, and Aysha, she demonstrates the active participation of women in both political and social life in contrast to pre-Islamic traditions. Nevertheless, the author also displays "how the veil fell upon Medina," how misogynist hadiths dismissed women from political life, and how liberationist attempts remained incomplete.[28] As Mernissi maintains, equality of the sexes is held as an exterior, "imported" phenomenon, rather than as an "interior, "inherent" one in society due to the "loss of memory" in the collective consciousness of Muslims.[29] Famous women are all allowed to be forgotten; "veiled," "enslaved," and "odalisque" (slave women at the service of the women of the harem) women have marked the image of Muslim women until today. Through the whole course of her study Mernissi points out the power relations that take place in the conflicting relationship between men and women in the Muslim communitites as the source of "misogynist hadiths." She completes her book with the following question: Why does a Muslim man need this wife, whose force is exhausted, to balance himself?[30]

The idea of the "degeneration of an ideal" is also explored in Abdel-wahab Bouhdiba's book *Sexuality in Islam*. In contrast to the books of canonical jurisprudence (*fikh*) and *sunna*, the Koran itself, he argues, does not bear any sign of misogyny.[31] He acknowledges the fact that there is inequality of status and of role differentiation between men and women in Islam. Yet, although the Koran established a hierarchical relationship within marriage, this division of labor works for the benefit of women.[32] As for the question of sexuality in Islam, he asserts that sexuality is the object of very special status in Islam, since it is an inevitable part of daily life and is the basic element of belief and love. According to his analysis, far from the repression and displacement of sexual desire, Islam suggests recognition of the body and satisfaction of the sexual desires.[33] On the other hand, none of the Koranic verses allows for a misogynist interpretation, though this cannot be said for many *sunnas* and *fikih* texts. He even postulates that Islamic civilization is fundamentally feminist, for, being a Muslim and a misogynist simultaneously are discordant. Nonetheless, as an outcome of the traditions that are harsh in their treatment of women, women's devaluation and dismissal in society have become defining characteristics of the Arabo-Muslim societies. In practice, the "principle of hierarchy between the sexes" dominates the "principle of complementarity."[34] The author concludes that the tie between the "morality of sexuality" assumed by Muslims and the Koran, as well as the hadiths of the Prophet, have been gradually weakened. The liberalizing attempts of Islam are again suffocated and deflected: "the roller wiped out all freshness and spontaneity that stepped in its track," writes Bouhdiba.[35] For this author, too, it is necessary to find the lost meaning of Islam.

All these statements and evaluations explaining the early Islamic period are meaningful so long as they constitute the basis of the Islamic social projects, leaving aside the question of how reflective of the "truth" they are. To put it differently, the social actors envision Islam in a new manner and transform the prevalent social movements with their reference to the Golden Age and their interpretations of the Koran. As maintained earlier, the myth of the Foundational period functioned as a utopia. But there exist many different ways of reappropriating the "lost meaning of Islam" and for their realization in the society. And this plurality translates into distinct political positions within the Islamic movement. The return of the Islamic movement to the sources—the Golden Age, the Koran—provides a ground for the utopian dimension of the movement and its realization in social life determines its ideological ramifications. The notion of utopia brings the untried, inexperienced, the almost unreasonable, to mind. This is exactly why it consists of a creative function; for utopia expresses the desire to transcend the current social reality, and it further draws the contours of this transcendence. An exiled society reinforces the idea of a countersociety and an alternative life, with its reminder of otherness and of a different place. Thus, Utopia has a function of novelty.

Placing the Golden Age in the lost but experienced past, as is the case for the Islamist movement, rather than in the future, as in the socialist utopia of the classless society, does not wipe out this "novelty" function of the utopia. The Islamist social movements direct their present-day activities by returning to the past and glorifying an "ideal" society, in short, the Islamic utopia. They struggle to put up with the contemporary modern world with the help of the strength they derive from their past. The issue here is not the denial of the modern world and its principles. The Islamic utopia serves as the reference point of an alternative lifestyle, which is brought into the scene against Western modernism. It is a perfect and conflict-free utopia that can be defined with the following principle: equality between human beings and the complementarity of the sexes are equivalents to harmony with nature and happiness. So far as the utopia is the project of an ideal society, it defines a world that is free of struggle and conflict and one that is self-reconciled. Nonetheless, as each social movement is nourished by a utopia, it is also armed with an ideology: the utopia feeds the idealism of the movement, and ideology, in turn, seeks the articulation of this idealism in social practice.[36] How, then, is the Islamic utopia expressed in current social relations? In general, it is possible to discern two distinct orientations: toward cultural Islam and toward political Islam.

Cultural Islam and Political Islam

Relying on the statement "the absence of an Islamic society lies beneath all these issues," the Islamic movement bases various ideologies and dynamics on the transfer of this utopia into modern society. The Islamic veiling movement embraces two distinct modes of action, one associated with political Islam, the other with cultural Islam. The former could possibly be defined as the "revolutionary" Islam that struggles against Western "imperialist" forces in order to defend Islamic identity and independence. It also gives priority to seizing power and defines "change" as a "top-to-bottom" process affecting the "system." This is not to say that cultural Islam lacks a political dimension. In cultural Islam it is the individual, not the state, who gains importance. Furthermore, the primary aim is not the constitution of a new system but, rather, the enclosure and transformation of inner worlds. The cultural Islamic orientation, then, seeks to protect Islam from the loss of its sacredness through profanation and from poverty through increasing politicization. Thus, in a sense the cultural orientation contributes to the constitution of an Islamic identity and determination of the transformative values and viewpoints of the society and individuals. The revolutionary political orientation, however, exerts itself at the political level against "the enemy" (i.e., the Western system). Thus, it is a typical revolutionary reaction of the Third World and of oppressed people generally. To elaborate, the Iranian case legitimized the politicization and revolutionization of Islam. Iran is cited as the first country that attempted to constitute a real Islamic community since the period of the Golden Age. By establishing an Islamic state, Iran provided a material base for the goal of Islamic *tebliğ*, the transmission of Islamic knowledge, and declared its Islamic identity and its independence from Western and imperialist forces. This situation proclaims and strengthens its revolutionary features. As an example of revolution, the Iranian model reinforced the political Islamism.[37] In contrast to political Islam, which presupposes the "political armament" and constitution of an Islamic state so as to ensure the re-Islamicization of society, cultural Islam gives priority to faith, religion, and the empowerment of the individual instead of politics and the state.

As set forth by Gilles Kepel, one can discern the differences between these distinct orientations with reference to the top-to-bottom Islamic revolutionary model and the bottom-to-top Islamicization attempts, in which the community itself plays a significant role. The top-to-bottom movement establishes the modus operandi of political Islamic movements, which basically advocates the exercise of the Sharia following the complete transformation of the society and is orientated toward the seizure of political power. As mentioned previously, the fundamental model of this is the Iranian revolution. As Kepel pointed out, however, starting in the 1980s a new model of Islamicization emerged, and the initial objective of this bottom-to-top mobilization was to cause a rupture in the daily life course of individuals along with constituting a base for the community, rather than seizing political power. The constitution of countercommunities and the transformation of the society from the bottom to top, both of which provide the elements of political mobilization, are the defining features of this new action's strategies.[38] As we shall see, it is cultural aspects that are most weighty in the bottom-to-top Islamicization movement.

Interviews held with two leading figures of the Islamic movement, Abdurrahman Dilipak and Ali Bulaç, throw light upon manifest differences between "political Islam" and "cultural Islam". Although both of them are from the radical Islamist movement, which favors a return to sources for the revival of Islam, they represent the two different dynamics of the Islamic movement. Starting from the premise that Islam is encircled by Western imperialism, Dilipak supports the prevalence of the political activities of the Islamic movements in order to lay the necessary conditions for the development of the Islamic society and of Muslim individuals. As distinct from this political figure of Islam, Ali Bulaç seeks an "alternative vision of the world" in Islam, arguing that "politicization" and "humanization" would lead to the impoverishment of Islam. To him, it is the search for an alternative vision concerning the relationships between technology and society, knowledge and truth, and human beings and nature that is important.

Political Islamism, in which the top-to-bottom course of change is predominant, is primarily concerned with the Islamic revolution and the type of state that would establish the system. Giving preeminence to political actions, this attitude expresses the reaction to order, attempts to bring about disorder through its activities, and takes credit for the conflict. Regardless of the fact that the "enemy" is defined in abstract terms (exterior forces, imperialism, the devil, etc.), the strength of the "opponent" functions as the movement's engine. The political orientation, which considers itself to be "encircled" and "oppressed" by the Western world, seeks to represent the Islamic actor and the values assumed by this actor. In contrast to political Islam, which advances confrontation with the "system," cultural Islam is the conveyor of a new value system. Laying the bases of the movement with the assistance of the "Muslim personality and identity," before all else it advocates "complete independence in the mental world."[39] Questioning the inherent tensions between Islam and politics, tradition and modernism, religion and profanity, belief and rationalist positivism, this movement locates the conflict between Islam and the West on a new intellectual axis.

Many Islamic thinkers attempt to stress the "distinctiveness" and "specificity" of Islam, regardless of the fact that they position themselves in different camps and cultural locations. They point to the fact that modernism surrounded even Muslim circles, and, in turn, they back an alternative vision of the world based on Islam. Among those who approach the politicization of Islam with a critical and dubious eye, İsmail Kara asserts that the notions of progress, secularism, and positivism have already dominated contemporary Islamic movements, and this phenomenon "rasps Islam." He argues that looking toward the period of the Golden Age allows for the "removal of the deflections" and the "return to the essences," whereas those Islamists who run after political power deal particularly with existing problems and enter into the domain of progressivists.[40] Similarly, he criticizes contemporary Islamic intellectuals who try to prove that Islam is compatible with science and rationality. On this basis he further argues that these intellectuals have become the "loyal and voluntary servants" of real secularism (in the sense of the profanation of life, relations, frames of thought, and even religion) and of positivism.[41] Assuming responsibility in the formation of a specific Islamic outlook with the effects of modernism removed, Kara prefers struggling to "remain Muslim" to the political confrontations that are held in the name of guaranteeing Islam's future.

Muslim intellectuals who oppose the "use of verses in the slogans" for the sake of profane power, and who replaced the *ulema* (religious) class of Ottoman society, seek to define "both Islam, which lies there to be saved, and the West, which stands there to be dismissed," according to Ruşen Çakır.[42] Paradoxically enough, Muslims who assume the specificity of the Islamic worldview are the ones who are indeed in pursuit of Western modernism and who simultaneously criticize this modernity. The antimodernist outlook developed in *Üç Mesele* (Three Issues), by İsmet Özel, the first Muslim intellectual to challenge the tendencies of profanation in Islam, is nourished by the cultural products of Western and Muslim thinkers.[43] As for the parallel lines of thought between particular Western frames of thought and the Islamic one, Nabi Avcı argues that "while we are according our instruments, that is, while we want to reach the best possible theoretical level, we are seen wandering on the same wavelength with them."[44] Following discussions on modernism, which come from within the Western world itself, Muslim intellectuals direct the magnetic needle toward the "apprehension of the world" rather than toward a politically "naive" reaction to the Western world.[45] Thus, they criticize traditional Islam and, at the same time, resist the siege of Islam by modernism. Discrediting both "traditionalism and conservatism, which were soiled by legends, and rationalism and positivism, which aim to interpret the Koran evasively with absolute reason and positivism," Ali Bulaç points to the *sunna*, which is able to integrate Muslim people all over the world in terms of their behavior, as the best means of resistance against modernism. He states that if the *sunna* is eradicated—that is, when it is possible for men to shake hands with women for the veil to be abandoned and for divine worship to be performed at any time and in any manner—then modernism will easily penetrate into the Muslim world and dictate its own institutions and customs.[46] The Islamic movement defines its difference (i.e., its otherness) from the Western world with regard to the submission of the individual to the sacred power, rituals of the companionship of women with men, and the matter of privacy/intimacy of the female body. Veiling themselves, women, who are symbols of the slaves' submission, the boundaries of intimacy (*mahrem*) between men and women, and of the forbidden zone, assume the role of conduit between Islam and secular, liberal Western modernism, which is established on removal of the prohibitions between the sexes and religion that is confined to its own sphere.

Nevertheless, the gender identity of women varies according to the two orientations of the Islamic movement. Political Islam puts forth the activist and "missionary" identity of women. The more the Islamic movement directs itself toward a revolutionary path, the more political radicalism reinforces the militant identity of women. To cite an example, *Mektup (Letter)*, a magazine popular among radical Islamic women who are supporters of complete veiling, published pictures of completely veiled women with *charshafs* using *kalashnikov* rifles, the symbol of all revolutions. Through images such as these the collective identity of women is defined, but their education finds support within the framework of the transmission of Islam, *tebliğ*. Emine Şenlikoğlu, the editor of *Mektup*, depicts this situation in her novel called *Bize Nasıl Kıydınız?* (How Did You Act Ruthlessly Against Us?). The main female character, Rabia, is a woman who initially works outside "among men" and even rides on buses with men in the middle of the night "in a state of undress." She gradually turns to Islam, abandons working, veils herself, and asks for a "companion in the service to the religion" for her marriage upon the *tebliğ* of her brother Hüseyin. Among the reasons for her marriage she cites the importance of a modest life ("I do not want expensive and fancy furniture . . . they should be as much as my needs"), her loyalty to the Islamic rules, her decision about veiling ("I wear old clothes, old shoes, but I never put on outdoor clothes which contradict Islam"), her submissiveness to her husband ("I will not go out without the permission of my husband"), and her decision not to reveal herself to any man but her husband ("I will not reveal myself to anybody except my *mahrem*, my husband"). Rabia is the antithesis of her sister, who admires the Western way of life and modern goods.[47] In her novel, in which the Islamic requirements assigned to men are also noted, Şenlikoğlu defines the ideal Muslim women as follows: "The Muslim women are not wiseacre, wasteful, slaves of fashion . . . They are not ashamed of obeying their husbands."[48]

An interview held with the well-known female Egyptian Islamic activist, Zaynab al-Ghazali, reveals the affinity between revolutionary Islam and traditional gender identities. She devotes herself to both the political and religious missions, and the priority given to her domestic roles slowed the development of her individual identity as a woman. Considering her first marriage as a barrier in her Islamic mission, Ghazali acknowledges that Islam does not act as an obstacle against women participating in political life or being involved in another activity, provided that this will not interfere with her motherhood responsibilities. Yet she reminds us that the preeminent missions and most holy responsibilities of a woman are motherhood and wifehood.[49]

As different from the traditional Muslim women, the revolutionary Islamic orientation maintains the activist-missionary identity of women. Nevertheless, radical Islam, too, falls short of questioning traditional gender relations, and, more or less, it reinforces these relations. The roles and responsibilities of women, rather than their individual identities, are taken into account in terms of their compatibility with Islam, and here women stand for loyalty to the Islamic social project. With the assistance of various publications this tendency attempts to introduce the "real Islam" to social groups with lower levels of education and culture who otherwise experience "folk Islam." Yet the discourses of "cheap radicalism and populism" lag behind rising renovationist Islamic interpretations.[50] Parallel to this, the Islamism of *Mektup* magazine and of Emine Şenlikoğlu was first criticized by Muslim intellectuals, and this Islamism was considered to be an amalgamation of "Islamicization and proletarianization," inclinations that signify the birth of an "Islamic arabesque."[51]

Social Practice

The revolutionary Islamic discourse that claims for women's rights under an Islamic society is nevertheless weakened once examined under the light of social practice. Political Islam, which assigns women the roles of "believer" and "missionary" on the path of belief and holy warfare, indeed defers the solutions to the everyday problems of women to the coming ideal Islamic society. Independent of the social reality constituting the experiences of women and men, political Islam is based upon references to the Islamic utopia of the past and the Islamic system of the future. Here it is useful to follow the encounter of this abstract idealistic discourse with women's social practices and to examine its relation to their concrete and everyday experiences.

Life Strategies

Behind the radical, collective, and political Islamic movement women have opted for developing life strategies so as to claim their individuality. It is likely that the political movement has enabled women to exit from the *mahrem* sphere to the public one. On top of this, regardless of its conservative attitude toward the position of women in society, the Islamic movement empowers women to claim their individual freedom—as seen in their participation in demonstrations organized to promote the right to veil as well as their involvement in publishing and in Koran meetings—as well as providing alternative lifestyles for them.[52]

University education also is quite influential in women's attempts to develop alternative life strategies. By means of education, they obtain more freedom in comparison to what they have had in their hometowns and in family circles, and thus they can postpone their marriages:

> My family in Eskişehir allows me to stay here because of my education. Or I can delay my marriage. But, in case I was enrolled in a Koran course, this would not stop them at all, and they could ask me to come back. Perhaps I don't want to be involved in family affairs before I feel I am a mature person. I don't know—maybe this is why I like studying.

Education is a means to broaden one's horizon and even to define oneself: "We are studying to widen our horizons, not to be confined to a limited world. In addition, studying provides a ground for self- definition."

Although from the standpoint of men in the Islamic movement education for women is considered to be an extension of their motherhood and religious tasks, for women it is the key element in their lives in terms of their maturation and process of individualization. Once the fixed ideologi-

cal arguments were left aside in the group discussion, the female participants felt free to express their own opinions, such as that education is an
individual need and is not related directly to becoming more learned:

> For me education is a question of humanity more than a religious phe-
> nomenon. That is to say, it doesn't mean that I separate religion from
> human beings, but we would probably want to study even if we were
> not Muslims. We would ask it because of our nature. We are not sup-
> posed to explain every conduct by religion; that is, you can't simply
> say that they study for religious *tebliğ*, for the religion, for the social
> status of religion.

For Muslim women, too, education is positioned on the natural curve of
life:

> While we were in the primary school, we wanted to attend the sec-
> ondary school, and the high school when we were in the secondary
> school, and now the university.

They were under strong pressure to prove their power of self-realization by
means of education as an outcome of the social class they come from and of
the Muslim identity they have assumed:

> Why shouldn't I study? The Muslims were always backward. For
> instance, I must be able to read foreign magazines to know what's
> going on abroad. This is my right. We are trying to prove ourselves, to
> show our self-realization.

The attempts at self-realization extend beyond the areas of education
and university, gatherings in the social sphere. Along with the step into the
world of education and employment, they create an autonomous zone for
themselves separate from both the domestic female identity and the
Islamist movement. Their longings for professional identity push the
boundaries of what Islam permits for education. In the end education turns
out to be an important step in their life strategies rather than a mere right
granted for achieving "better ways of raising children or more effective
ways of transmitting Islam."

Thus, a number of different attitudes emerged in the group discussion
toward women's work. According to the first attitude, the main task of

women is motherhood; thus, education is pursued not as a means to work necessarily but, rather, as a tool for raising children in a better way. This attitude was raised particularly by a magazine editor in the group, who was older than the rest of the discussion participants and more "enlightened" than other members of the group; her argument was generally welcomed by the group. The second attitude was raised by a male interlocutor of the group, and it reminded female participants about their religious tasks. As he put it, the main responsibility of educated women is to transmit Islam. Opposing these two attitudes, however, was a third one, expressed by the group members with regard to the assumption of professional identities. The determined voice of a medical school student who was opposed to the idea that women pursue education so as to raise their children properly or to transmit Islam in fact argued for the connection between education and professionalization:

> You have just said that, before all, a Muslim woman is supposed to serve her family. Of course, this is true. But, I want to be useful to people around me as well. It now seems as if we study only for *tebliğ*. . . . Let's say that one of us wants to become a woman gynecologist. For sure, she wants to be useful to her patients. She wants to work as a gynecologist, and she wants to treat them.

The idea of women's work was raised initially with reference to its social benefits. As the group participants claimed, they wanted to become doctors, pharmacists, and teachers, and they further claimed that this would be accomplished in order to serve Muslim women and society. Yet this attitude was later formulated in a more radical fashion when it was argued that Islam does not forbid women from working and that women may well prefer the world of public life and education to motherhood; this preference was a question of personal choice:

> Islam is open to interpretation. A woman may think that her motherhood tasks come before anything else. For this woman the best thing in life is taking care of her children and staying at home. She can interpret Islam in this way. I look at Islam and say that since Islam is such a religion where women, too, can participate in the social and economic life, and it does not outlaw all these explicitly—what I am saying here is that it does *not* forbid these, this is not a suggestion—then I will study . . . That is to say, the condition where some women con-

sider themselves only as mothers and where the rest find their existence outside the house . . . springs from the flexible order of Islam, which fulfills every individual's needs.

Along with their expression of willingness to participate in the social life, Muslim women do not want to restrict their female identity to motherhood responsibilities. They leave the *mahrem* sphere behind by means of education and political activity, and they find themselves in the classroom, on the road, in the bus, and in all other urban settings—that is, the mutually shared life spaces of urban settlements. Their social practice pushes Islamic discourse to its limit. Their individualized life strategies embody seeds of potential conflict within Islamic circles and especially with men.

Conflict with Men

One of the outstanding representatives of Islamic discourse was invited to the group discussion along with his wife. He expressed his will "to provoke women to defend their rights" and he presented his Islamic viewpoint, in which the definition of *human being* lies in the center, disregarding the question of gender:

> I do not see any question of gender; we are all human beings. But, for the maintenance of life, we are created in different sexes . . . I suppose that through time men preferred to use their physical strength to direct women in the way they wish. Because wealth and the arms were at their hands, and they occupied the power.

The speaker defines himself as a Muslim man who defends the rights of women granted by Islam. In conversation he used radical Islamic interpretive methods which refer to the written texts rather than experienced "traditional" Islamic practices:

> I think that women have moved away from their revelation responsibilities. I want them to reclaim their God-given rights from whoever possessed them and whoever seized them.

Although he admitted that knowledge is an "obligation for both men and women" and that men's needs are the needs of women as well, once the question of women's work was considered, he proclaimed that it is against the nature of women and Islamic rules, and he even contended that it results in "environmental pollution."

> [She] cannot adopt any behavior or attitude which would overshadow her motherhood qualifications. For this is an environmental pollutant; that is, it is a phenomenon of alienation, alienation against nature, which occurs outside the natural balance of human beings.

He set down restrictions on women's work with reference to the "natural qualifications" of women, with the claim that they "cannot dispose their knowledge with a self-possessed attitude" and "this [knowledge] must be used for the benefits of human beings in *tebliğ*." He displayed the religiopolitical mindset attributed by political Islam and utilized its essentialist definitions. Women are confined to their traditional mother and wife roles in the house and in their relations with their husbands with the support of essentialist arguments, yet within the context of their religious and political activities their increasing level of education is tolerated. Militant in society and traditional in the private sphere is the idealized image of women as held by political Islamism. Education of women is tolerated only if it serves for the collective political cause of Islam or for the education of children in the family.

Nevertheless, women question this ideal image. Muslim women expressed their opposition to the statements of this Islamic leader when they declared that men do not realize their "revelation" responsibilities either, and, if they had done so, it would have been easier for women to reconcile their motherhood tasks and work life:

> For a woman to be a mother is not an obstacle to reaching a knowledge and science. Women can do both of these at the same time. However, when they give birth to children, then the issue of care emerges. But, why should it be only her responsibility? It is an obligation for men, too.

The will of women to participate in social life, along with fulfilling their motherhood tasks, provides a ground for dispute between Muslim men and women. The members of the discussion group supported the statements of the male "leader" so as to prove to the sociologist that men respect the rights of women in the religion of Islam. Yet it is quite striking that the demand of Muslim women that men share their motherhood tasks runs parallel to what Western feminists demand on the same issue.[53]

The emerging conflict between Islamic men and women is intended to be transcended by reference to the Golden Age of Islam. As maintained previously, the idea that "once Islam dominates completely over the society, all problems will be solved" is expressed in Islamic political discourse. Imagining the ideal Islamic society, the speaker discussed the problems experienced by women—and suggested that they could be ameliorated with the assistance of the state:

> To live Islam at this level is something and to live it at another is something else. . . . In Islamic society my wife is not even supposed to suckle my child. . . . I will find the wet nurse. In addition, the state must organize the requirements and obligations of religion.

Along with the male guest, the group members found shelter in Islamic ideology by referring to the Golden Age and cited enthusiastically how women in the Golden Age were involved in social activities and traded with their own accumulated capital, while their children were taken care of by others; they claimed that once Islam started to be exercised all the problems of women will be eliminated. But the magic of utopia diminished when the sociologist asked the speaker's wife how she organizes her own life with her children. The group members once again became aware of the difference between utopia and the experienced reality. The female guest described her life vividly without any comprehensive and ideological "lecture" on Islam:

> I have three children, but . . . my husband is really fond of children and wants more. Since he works so much, all responsibilities for them are on my shoulders. So, naturally, I have to sacrifice quite a lot. I have almost no social life. I made many plans in my mind last night just to come here—where I should leave children, what I should do. And, of course, I left my mind at home. I would be very much pleased if this problem were to be solved. Well, my oldest child is very helpful, so I suppose I'm very lucky. I wish this could be easier, and I would have more of a social life; I would be free of a monotonous life. Naturally, I want to participate in social life, and I want to be more active.

This modest but very determined involvement in the discussion in fact verbalizes the life strategies and yearnings of women behind the discourse of an idealized Islamist society. Although she is part of the radical Islamic movement herself, this woman speaks for the problems of all women as mothers who want to be involved in social action, instead of a tautological discourse, regardless of whether they are Muslims or not. Her opinion was taken into consideration carefully by the group members due to her position in the social movement. In other words, her opinion could not be criticized on the grounds that either she or her husband is one of those "ignorant and traditional Muslims." They are the "ideal" figures of radical Islam. And, above all, her husband is a supporter of Muslim women's rights in the Islamic movement.

With this intervention it became possible in the group for women to freely express the will to participate in social life, and for the ideological attitude that says motherhood tasks are primary to be weakened. Nonetheless, the ideological fracture exists and brings about political resistance. The Islamic women accepted the "political solution"—that is, the primacy of the constitution of an Islamic system—as supported by the male speaker. Criticizing working conditions in contemporary society, they stated that it is full-time work itself that limits the freedom of women, contrary to our expectations, and they moved closer toward an approach that gave priority to changing the system before taking the question of work into consideration. The male speaker, however, insisted on arguing that the Islamic system would overcome these issues:

> I suggest a political solution. . . . For example, my wife says that we should establish an association to defend veiling. Well, I'll be somewhere, and you'll be somewhere else, and, if we work till the morning, this will sweep away our family, as I told her. Because, I have some extra work. . . . There exist two systems of law in Islam: countries outside the domain of Islam and countries in the dominion of Islam. Today in this system our behavior is different. In the Islamic system there would not be any problems. The state, or more truly, the community, would organize itself. . . . There would be so many established foundations where women could leave their children and participate in social activities.

This Islamic man not only supported the traditional premises that argued that the integrity of family depends on the position of women in the family but also supported the shared belief of all revolutionaries, whether Islamic or leftist: all problems will be solved after the revolution.

Nevertheless, this discourse, which postpones all the issues to be solved until after the revolution, came loose within the reality of everyday experiences for this couple. The discussion that took place between the spouses, with witty remarks, designates the limits of the political discourse. Political Islam falls short in the identity struggle of women. In the meantime, following the expression of the will to participate in social life, the woman took a further step when she points out the necessity and principle of sharing within familial life and mentions her own dissatisfaction with her husband, who does not fulfill his fatherhood responsibilities: "For example, I oppose his candidacy in the elections. Because the children start to ask me, 'Where is our father?' The children can't see their father." The friction between the invited couple turned into a private one. Trying to express himself as freely as his wife, the man challenged the feminist attitudes of women when he mentioned sarcastically what he says to his wife: " 'So, you will become feminist,' and she regards this as an insult." All humor aside, feminism seems to play an important role in the formation of Islamic female identity.[54]

Feminism

Discussions on feminism published in the daily *Zaman* throw light on the nature of tensions and conflicts taking place unexpectedly between women and men in the Islamic movement. Following an article that criticized feminism, Ali Bulaç, among the representatives of the cultural Islamic outlook, found himself the target of an attack by Islamic women. The women, who support women's rights, opposed ideas presented in this article, and published a series of articles in *Zaman*. This dispute, in a sense, reveals the attempts and struggles of Islamic women to be able to participate in social life and develop independent personalities.

The introduction of Ali Bulaç's article "Feminist Bayanların Kısa Aklı" (The Short Intelligence of Feminist Women) acknowledges the demands of the early feminist movement by recognizing women's exploitation by the capitalist system, which treats them as second-class citizens. Nevertheless, he argues that in contemporary Western welfare societies certain social issues, such as low pay and bad working conditions, do not exist anymore and men are subject to the devastation of modernity as much as women are. The author contends that the issues brought about by modernity, including technology, production, and alienation, are no longer only the problems of women; they have become issues for all humanity, and the feminist movement has lost its oppositionary power in the society. As far as "undeveloped societies like [Turkey's]" are concerned, Bulaç concludes that there is no need for feminism: "Well, what about us ? In our history and culture, women were never treated with contempt, and they were not degraded at all. They were not forced to work at factories all day long like slaves; they were not left in need of bread in the streets of *gecekondus* and their honor was not sold."

Suggesting that "skewed industrialization and modernism" has contributed to the objectification of women, he maintains that it is the act of veiling, not feminism, that appears as the "noble rebel" of women against this objectification. He considers feminism as a movement in the "service to modernism," which even "asks women to rebel against men" and results in the "deterioration of the relationship between men and women." As argued by Bulaç, if feminism becomes a way of life, then the conflict between men and women will lead to the emergence of hatred and anxiety in the relations between the two sexes. If this happens, Bulaç contends that humanity will no longer be able to maintain its existence because of the fact that "the only possible form of sexual relation left will be either homosexuality or lesbianism." Condemning feminism as a movement hostile to men and conducive to homosexuality, the author concludes his article with the following words: "Feminist ladies, you have limited minds and your feet are not on the ground." With this conclusion he finds the feminist and the veiled Islamic women's movements in opposition in Turkey.[55]

Nevertheless, women were distressed by the devaluation of Western feminism and the glorification of the Islamic movement. Six months after the publication of Bulaç's article Islamic women addressed the controversy with a series of ironic responses. Mualla Gülnaz's article "Ali Bulaç'ın Düşündürdükleri" (What Ali Bulaç Evoked) expresses sympathy for feminism:

> I learned of its [Bulaç's article] publication on the World Women's Day. I was startled when I asked the newspaper agent whether there is the issue of *Feminist* magazine. . . . I knew that they [Turkish feminists] were aware of the contemptuous people in this society, and they were disapproving this; they were offended, hurt, yet at the same time, brave women and I wanted to know who they are. And, of course, they were really intelligent! On the same day I read Ali Bulaç's article "Feminist Bayanların Kısa Aklı."

In her article Gülnaz acknowledges that patriarchal oppression is not unique to capitalist society at all, and it is widespread in all societies, so she challenges Islamic history and the cultural thesis of Bulaç:

Patriarchal oppression is a phenomenon . . . existing along with capitalist or socialist oppression. Our history and culture are influenced by this oppression to a large extent. . . . It is just a big lie that women are not devalued in this region. . . . I am not aware that our history and culture that refers to a golden age when egalitarian rules predominated.

The article challenges men with its definition of feminism as a movement targeting the liberation of women in both social and domestic life. It also touches upon the argument that men are scared of feminism solely because it threatens their oppressive attitudes:

Yes! Feminism invites women to rebel against the domination of men. In the house, at work, in the street. What's the use of fear from this so much? . . . Isn't it possible to leave oppressive attitudes instead of insisting to play with the words? . . . We must accept that it is really difficult to give up habits, habits that are so enjoyable.[56]

Another article, written by Tuba Tuncer entitled "Kimin Aklı Kısa?" (Whose Intelligence Is Short?), points out the "lowbrow" mistreatment of feminism such as equating it with "sexual freedom" and the "cause of lesbianism." The article responds to Ali Bulaç by proclaiming feminism as a movement "against the sexual exploitation of women." Tuncer argues that the main concern of women is not "sharing the same bed with men" but, rather, "struggling for equality with them," and she speaks for all women when she asserts that "women do not come into this world only to raise children and assume household tasks" and that "they are not less intelligent than men." Taking one more step, she disagrees with the attitude of men who push for women's veiling, and she expects women to speak for themselves. Thus, she rejects the attempts to initiate a conflict between feminists and Islamic women:

It is impossible to defend the veiling of our girls by announcing some women as the enemy. It is quite meaningful that the veil is defended more strongly by men than by those who wear it.[57]

Although both Gülnaz and Tuncer are from the radical Islamic movement, they are not satisfied with what the Islamist ideology provides women. Depending upon the daily experiences and social position of women, they demand the autonomy and development of women both at the collective and personal levels. They lean toward the raising of women's consciousness at the expense of positioning themselves against Islamic men rather than feminists.

Another *Zaman* article written by Elif H. Toros and entitled "Feminist Kime Derler?" (Who Is Feminist?), deplores the radical and skeptical outlook in the approach of Islamic men toward the question of women. This article, which argues that the confinement of women to their homes in the name of protection only serves to fulfill men's needs, views the oppression of women from within the framework of existing gender relations in Turkey, rather than with reference to Western civilization or the capitalist system:

> The woman is expected to conform to the image of a woman relegated to a protective sphere. . . . Except for wifehood and motherhood, she does not hold any responsibility. Thus, she ought to stay home to protect herself from malice. . . . She must keep her feet firmly on the ground so that a man, whose one foot is in the banks, public transport vehicles, schools, pavements, offices, may be able to reveal his consciousness with the other foot, to feel Islam. Since he lacks the power to change himself. . . . before he expresses himself. . . . he oppresses women.

The article argues that feminism uncovers the fact that the "wheels of men operate against women," and their struggles for women's rights:

> Those women who are aware of this and those who claim their share occupied by men are feminists, and their goal is . . . to call women to solidarity against men . . . Thus, the feminist movement is the struggle of women to prove to men, who monopolized the world, their "humanity. " Or the fact that they can leave them. Alone.[58]

What is underscored in this passage is not the equality of men and women, which is among the main objectives of feminism. Muslim men are pointed out as the main reason for women's oppression and the limitation of their life spaces to domestic roles. For the Islamic movement the totality of Islamic morality is dependent on the loyalty of women to familial roles. This Islamic approach, which lays down the bases of women's position in the society, has been elaborated by Bouhdiba. According to him, the Arabic women assumed the role of "guardian of the traditions and protector of the collective identity." A man who conforms to the new order outside, however, "finds himself in the perpetuation of the past" when he is back home.[59]

As witnessed, while men enjoy the benefits of the modern world, Islamic women do not easily accept confinement of their lives to domestic roles. These women reveal the fact that it is not the religion but the interests of Muslim men themselves that lay beneath the "advice" given to women in the name of religion. Thus, the women who participated in this research object to the differentiation of men and women in the practice of Islam:

> They try to isolate women from the society by posing unlawful situations. For example, a Muslim man does not allow his wife to attend a school, to work, and to get on buses. They always remember the unlawful cases when women are concerned. . . . If I am in a position of disobedience of Allah's rules, they must be valid for men, too . . . It is unlawful for him as well to get on a bus.

The Islamic women who do not apprehend why they have to play the roles of "renunciator and sacrificer" further question men of the Islamic movement:

> It is such an easy solution for men to ask women, who want to fulfill the requirements of a social being, "to give up their needs and desires since they are all unlawful!"[60]

This demanding process of women's questioning receives the expected response. The Islamic men who write in *Zaman* under the titles of "professor" and "doctor" touch upon the distinctive nature of women with the use of "the power of science," and they further attempt to legitimize women's domestic positions by reminding them of their motherhood tasks. Islamic men often use the archetypes of "strong man" and "childish woman," "emotional woman" who needs to be "protected."[61] On the whole they claim that men are extroverted, active, and have the will to conquer the outside world, while women have an intrinsically introverted nature and are dominated by emotions; they are "in between a child and a man."

Islamic men further proclaim that the "domestic position" of women is just an extension of their "introverted" nature. Consequently, they try to locate the discussion on a new platform, freeing it from the issue of power relations, which rests on "biological" (thus, inevitable), since it is based on the nature of women, and "scientific" (thus, unquestionable) arguments. On top of this they criticize women for referring to Western feminists and the women's question in Islam, which is claimed to be free of oppressive attitudes.

Nonetheless, once women are reminded about their "positions and responsibilities" in such a way, they take on the issue of their motherhood tasks. In an article entitled "Kadınlar Yine Kadındır" (Women Are Still Women), Tuncer maintains that the very definition of femininity cannot be limited to motherhood, and she objects to the stigmatization of women, like herself, who write articles in the newspaper, as masculine women. The author further questions the roles assigned to women as well as the power relations operating between men and women when she asserts that "men take refuge in science to imprison women at home," and beyond that, they "mystify motherhood roles." She points out that women who dedicate themselves to their motherhood role develop neurotic obsessions about either their children or cleanliness:

> Does maternal love mean threatening to abandon her children, screaming hysterically and accusing them of torturing her, evoking feelings of guilt? . . . For a woman who spends most of her life at home to keep her house clean becomes the main concern. . . . the children become the victims of the cleanliness and order obsessions of their mothers.[62]

Islamic women violate another taboo in their attempts at defining their female identities as individuals when they question the overvaluation of child-mother relations. They reveal the power relations between the sexes and claim that it is indeed the men who fear the struggle of Muslim women to assume their individualism:

> Why are Muslim men so afraid of the educated and learned women? Because it is so easy to dominate, appeal to and subjugate those women who lost contact with the world and are concerned only with the house. Once women start to better themselves with education and hold a critical eye, they then scare men. The character of a con-senting, obedient, and "sleeping beauty" woman is so charming indeed![63]

Islamic women writers point to the contradiction of men thinkers of Islamism, who use references to Western thinkers while criticizing Muslim women's interest in Western feminism.

> With the same course of logic it is possible to question why Muslim men take the environment as a social issue. . . . If this logical reasoning is maintained, then Muslims will not have any issue. . . . Why can't they tolerate our reference to Betty Friedan, for instance, while the Muslim circles can refer to Popper, Kuhn, and they can adopt similar discourse of the Western alternative movements or benefit from them?[64]

In the meantime Muslim men pose severe criticisms, and the "outstanding figures" of the movement even ask writers to halt this controversy; one of the daily newspapers has been accused of "organizing an illegal feminist page," and the female authors are blamed for "apostasy," "betrayal," and "infidelity to Islam." One of the journalists from *Zaman* published an article called "Davaya İhanet Edenler" (The Betrayers of the Struggle), in which the author regrets to state that all the letters of accusation came from men, who are reluctant to "weaken their masculinity, which is constructed on power and repression," and he also asserts that the gendered identity that is socialized in this vein "provides a ground for the flourishment of fascism"; he invites all men to think over this issue.[65]

Once again the overlapping affinity between politics and the relations between the sexes appears. The questioning attitudes of women are not limited to the existing relations between men and women; they determine the course of the Islamic movement's orientation. The cultural Islamic orientation, too, which reduces the scope of the movement to the question of "human being" instead of the "system" and which defines its relations with the Western world in terms of "interaction" rather than "reaction," becomes subject to the transformative forces of intellectual Muslim women in their process of individuation.

Personality but Not Femininity

The Islamic utopia or philosophy of the return to the Golden Age, on the one hand, frees the radical Islamist movement from traditional definitions and, on the other, struggles to overcome modernism. The more the Islamist sources are returned to, the more the definitions of human rights are provided, and the more the principle of equality finds a space in the radical Islamic movements. Yet this "return" may well be equated with the rejection of the question of women at the same time. This is so particularly because of the fact that, once the ideal Islamist system is realized in the society, it will be claimed that both men and women assume the same rights—as much as their natures permit. Today women are expected to cling to their "believer" and "missionary" roles. Thus, the question of women from the standpoint of radical Islam is rejected by reducing it to a question of Western societies. Nevertheless, this abstract discourse regarding the happiness of women, which originates in the Islamic utopia, is tested in the daily experiences of women. References to feminism designate all systems, whether they are capitalist, socialist, or Islamist, as male dominated. Islamic women give up postponing their demands to the ideal Islamist system of the future and locate their everyday experiences and male-dominated relations which are interwoven with sacred rules, at the very center of their questions. They point to the power assumed by men behind women's confinement to the houses in the name of their "fragile nature" and the "unlawful world of modernism." Hence, they start questioning the power relations embedded in the Islamic community along with their demand for participation in social life.

In the meantime, Islamic women have begun to redefine the Muslim female identity by their entrance into the social sphere. References made to feminism support their definitive transition from the position of being "objects" to that of being "subjects." They struggle to survive as objects, leaving behind their identities which depend on others—including being, the symbol of the Islamic movement, the wives of men, and the mothers of children. Hence, the radical Islamist movement has enabled women to emerge as collective social actors. Women strengthen their positions by attaining collective identity and their consciousness by means of politics. They highlight the differences between men and women, infringing on the transgender "human being" definition of cultural Islam. Meanwhile, the feminist movement contributes to the formation of women's consciousness and it reveals the dimension of gender embedded in power relations.

Women uphold a female identity independent of men and children as individual female beings and demand a "private sphere" for themselves:

> What we want to state is that a woman must have an identity of her own independent of being a wife of man and mother of children.[66]

No, a woman must have her own life. . . . She must not interfere in other private lives. She must not give up her own life when she gives birth to a child.[67]

They oppose the so-called protective attitude of Islam, which serves the interests of men rather than of women. Therefore, they identify Muslim men, instead of the Western world or traditions, as the main source of oppression and domination of women. In other words, the Islamic women's movement carries the potential for transforming the patterns of social life based on women's own experiences. In line with cultural Islam, they start with human beings, yet they take one step back and base the movement within the sphere of *mahrem*. This forbidden, traditional realm, which resists time, is brought into the picture and made part of the political sphere by women.

"Well what do we want? We want the Muslim women to reveal themselves; the society and the streets are not more dangerous to women than they are to men!"[68] The point here is that Muslim women have started to gain visibility in public life regardless of the fact that they are concealed behind turbans and long overcoats. They try to withdraw from the traditional life patterns of women that await them unless the limits of their life paths are questioned. They can attain a social identity so long as they are able to get rid of the conventional definitions of "femininity." Their traditional background gives them images of the lifestyles of women in detail and provides the definition of a "woman they do not want to be like":

A great number of women who have "feminine" preoccupations queue in front of the tombs, devote their innovative activities to new cake recipes, to knit different sorts of tablecloths, to spend their times at reception or *mevlüt* days.[69]

The book *Tanımsız (Undefined)*, by Halime Toros, which is among the best examples of attempts to provide a new language to women, starts with a criticism of the traditional middle-class woman's life, from which Islamist women aim to detach themselves. "We wanted to draw the attention to those Muslim women who are forgotten in the houses. . . . we are supposed to object initially to our defined position and identities, for all the factors which mute us are embedded in this definition," writes Toros. She states her objective as follows: "to render women a language . . . [free from] the harassment of given images and surrounded lives . . . to cast off our social stammering."[70]

Thus, monotonous everyday life made up of constantly crying children, indifferent husbands, neighbors who prepare tomato sauce at home, strong foul smells, and the weariness, rage, and desperation evoked in women by the married life that has lost all of its excitement are among the topics touched on in her story. The radical Islamic identity they expose expresses and reinforces their desire to free themselves from this monotonous life and their willingness to be different: "You would stroke your veil gently, wander around a bit, and go back to your home, since you are different or you want to be different from those who take a drink at Sakarya after work or who admire showy shop windows."[71]

By the means of veiling, women try to free themselves from the given conventional patterns of life and yet to differ from traditional Muslim women. Veiling, which represents submission to God's orders, in fact reinforces the alteration of the consciousness. Paradoxically enough, Islam, the community religion, provides a basis for the identity transformation initiated at the level of the individual consciousness.

The veil contributes to positioning women in the modern world as much as it serves the inner transformation of women against the monotonous worlds that mute them, and it further functions as a lever in the search for identity. The veil protects them against modernism and symbolizes their loyalty to Islam. The veil conceals the departure of Muslim women to the outside world, for, although the veiled women are in the outside world, they still remain in the "inside," and the veil constantly reminds them that they belong to the *mahrem* sphere.[72] In the face of modern women who exhibit their femininity by the care they give to their bodies and clothes, Muslim women conceal their femininity behind veiling and thus present the "sacred body" against the "aesthetic" one. They once again mark their difference from Western modernism. Veiled women, like their predecessors, enter into public life with the slogan "Personality but Not Femininity."[73]

CHAPTER 5

Conclusion

The Dark Side of Modernism

Once the reading of Islamic movements' meanings is broadened past the level of politics and the details of social life are further pursued, then it is easy to see traces of social change and cultural breaking points beyond the signs of "reactionism" that these movements evince. Thus, when the system of meaning embedded within the Islamic movements is taken as the main theme of inquiry, it becomes possible to move from a macro-level analysis of historical modernism to a micro-level explication of the everyday experiences of individuals. While politicized Islam provides the reading of the social history of Turkey with a new paradigm, the question of women maintains its privileged position in illuminating the social transformation taking place at the levels of both historicism and everyday life. For it is still women who emerge as the touchstone not only of the historical transformation bound up with the project of modernity, but also of the Islamic social structure, which rests upon the segregation of the sexes. To elaborate, as much as the production of central social values is contingent upon the social position women hold, the formation of basic spheres of life likewise is dependent on women's roles. That is to say, it is around the issue of the visibility of women that the frontiers between the private (*mahrem*) sphere and the public one are drawn, as is the case with the embodiment of modern values identified with the Western world. It is even arguable that the consciousness of the public (i.e., a new consciousness and social aggregation—what Hegel terms "civilized society"), which was not visible in Ottoman society, emerged as a consequence of defining women as "human beings" and their socialization along with Turkish modernization.[1] When it is stated that women are the symbols of the civilization project, what is actually meant is that it is women who sowed the field and enabled the planting of seeds of early consciousness with regard to the public sphere. Women fostered the increasing visibility of this sphere, regardless of the fact that "national" values still superseded "individual" ones in the Turkish case.

The course of Turkish modernization redefined central social values and even the concept of "human" in light of the influences of Western civilization. Western modernism, which was bred according to the premises of the Enlightenment and industrial civilization, transformed communitarian relations which had been molded by religious and traditional beliefs, and eventually produced a heterogeneous, differentiated, and pluralistic social structure that contributed to the formation of rationalist and positivist as well as liberal values. Turkish modernism, on the other hand, refused to recognize autonomous spheres in the market and civil society and was based on state authoritarianism. Turkish nationalism fears liberalism and pluralism as disintegrating forces. Neo-Kemalism's incessant mistrust of the market economy in the name of "national interests," liberalism, and individualism, to which it finds itself unaccustomed, are the indicators of the adverse position nationalist ideology maintains against the majority of the civil society. It won't be an exaggeration to set forth liberalism, fundamentalism, Kurdism, and communism as four fundamental phobias of Turkish nationalism, all of which represent autonomous spheres outside the state's domain. In short, Turkish modernism is not built upon the entrepreneurial or innovative forces of civil society, which rest upon principles of differentiation and plurality. On the contrary, it is a project of civilization by which local patterns and traditional values are dismissed and devalorized. As a consequence, within the framework of this civilization project, local Islam, which is considered as alien to rationalist and positivist values, is expelled, put outside the realm of history. Beyond the political and economic classifications the "civilization" project of the elites has penetrated into the sphere of what Pierre Bourdieu calls *habitus*, which operates beneath the levels of consciousness and language and which functions outside one's own will yet determines one's manner of eating, acting, speaking, and so on.[2] The distinction between the "civilized" person and the "Muslim" refers to this tacit realm of conflict in which new social distinctions and social stratification take place.

The contemporary Islamist movement recreates the Muslim identity, erased in the collective memory by modernism, in a collective vein and turns it into a social actor. This process, which has accelerated since the 1980s, in fact began, along with the formation of civil society, in the 1950s. Behind the political rise of the Islamist movements lies the upward mobility of new social groups and their increasing social participation. This is exactly why it would be a crude reductionism to analyze the Islamist movements as the movements of those groups that are uneducated, unemployed, or, at least, without promising futures, when the Turkish case is taken into consideration. Along with the radical Islamist movements a new profile of urban and educated Muslim identity has emerged. What is now taking place is the formation of Islamic intellectuals and elites who are educated, upwardly mobile, and urbanized, appearing in the modern settings of major cities and the provinces and participating in the formation of normative values, thus, affecting the direction of social change.

Once it is remembered that the "cultivated/enlightened" person of the Kemalist project of civilization was strongly influenced by Western manners and rituals of behavior, then it becomes much more plausible to argue that the Islamic actors, in a sense, have altered the definition of historical agency with their subversion of the identification between Westernized and "civilized" person. On the one hand, Islamism legitimizes Muslim identity and empowers Muslims as political agents of historical and cultural change. On the other hand, new Islamic actors, as they reappropriate modernity, challenge the Westernist mode of modernism. In other words, Muslim actors enter the historical stage through the Islamist gate, and once they are actors on the stage, an interplay is engaged between "Muslim" and "modern."

It is quite meaningful to observe that the new upwardly mobile social groups refer to Islamic values in forming their life strategies. This phenomenon in fact epitomizes the dissociation between elites, who hope that society continues moving toward Western civilization, and the upwardly mobile social groups which maintain their existence on the strength of local values when the historicity of society is not produced intrinsically. To put it crudely, the cultural and social dissociation between Westernist elites and the Muslim people is an integral part of Turkey's weak historicity. For modernity is defined with reference to a civilization project, which stands for the attainment of Western ways of life rather than for the strength of local class dynamics and the transformation of traditions.[3] In contrast to that of the Western world, Turkish modernism did not derive its definition from the evolution of local values and social patterns. Şerif Mardin argues that Turkish modernization "could not transform the low-brow culture'" and, for instance, did not produce "new literary genres"; on the other hand, it has become useless for modern democracy, thanks to the "narcissism, sterility and discriminatory outlook" of the elite culture.[4] Underlying the persistent dissociation between the "ornamented language and values" of the "ruling class" and "popular culture" and the "living language" of the countryside since the Ottomans, Mardin maintains that, with the onset of democratization (i.e., since the second half of the 1940s), elements of the "small traditions" gradually penetrated the realm of "grand tradition."[5] Hence, it is this reality that lies beneath the frequently heard complaints such as "the cities are ruralized" and "arabesque culture has besieged us." Turkish society has evolved toward modern settings and new forms of life, yet remains a foreigner to the manners of the Kemalist project of civilization. The values put forward by the Westernist elites fail to fulfill the expectations of new rising classes and to provide codes of behavior and social guidance. It is even the case that the current elitism is transmuted in the direction of neo-Kemalism, which stands in opposition to the "parvenu" rising classes as well as the "invasion of Anatolian countryside culture," represented in both arabesque and Islamic cultures, given voice by the Motherland Party during the 1983–1993 decade.

It now is useful to note the replacement of the nation's identification of Western civilization with European experiences with its aspiration for American cultures since the beginning of the 1950s. Thus, recently, rising classes have adopted the American "intimiste" and "democratic" lifestyle. European culture, which is more rigid, no longer acts as a model for Turkish society, which has undergone a rapid process of evolution. Turkish society, which has encountered the power of money and new patterns of consumption, particularly since the 1980s, seeks new codes of behavior. "Anarchic" market individualism, which subverted the existing cultural and economical hierarchies in society, is an example of this claim. Another example comes from the widespread interest of people from the upper classes in the clothing styles of the residents of the *gecekondu* squatters districts. As a result of this interest, sweatsuits have become a transcultural and transclass form of clothing in Turkish society. The sweatsuit has become an extension of the "slipper culture" in Turkey, as well as a subversion of the boundaries between interior house space and exterior urban space.

The consciousness and rituals associated with urban and public spaces are part of a European tradition. Thus, urban settings, which for a long time have been organized on the basis of cultural and class hierarchy, witness every detail of society's customs and manners. The recently observed "nostalgia" of Beyoğlu, a district in Istanbul, in fact is a potent reminder of the uprootedness of "European" manners (indeed, the definition of civilization), in the relationship between people and urban settings;

ladies with gloves and hats and gentlemen with suits, who are clean shaven, represent the culture in which the consciousness of public space is rooted. As a matter of fact, it is disputable how far they have renewed themselves or resisted the intimate style associated with contemporary European cultures.[6] Thus, the transgressive extension of the private sphere into the realm of the public seems to be a common experience for all societies.[7] In fact, the sturdiest element of the public realm, that is, politics, is increasingly subject to the processes of "individuation" and "transparency."[8] As much as with the politicization of genders, certain issues of the *mahrem* (the private realm), such as abortion, veiling, and violence against women, have moved into the public arena and the mass media. According to Foucault, Western civilization was established on confession; the most difficult things to mention are verbalized explicitly, and desires, wishes, and secrets are revealed. Confession has become one of those inevitable rituals of life, an element in the very formation of reality and hegemony.[9] Once the relations of power become rooted in the formation of social reality at micro-levels and when, as a consequence, the sources of repression are hard to detect, then the role symbols play in political discourse gains greater significance. The body then becomes a symbol of resistance as much as of power relations.[10]

This argument supports the claim that the veiled body of Islamic women represents resistance against the abstract hegemony of Western civilization over social manners. Western modernism takes the human body in the spiral of secularization and aims to increase the domination of human willpower over the body. Hence, the performance of the body appears to be responsible for the health, energy, and dynamism of any individual. Sports, habits of eating and drinking, physical appearance, physical energy, become the new criteria of privilege and superiority among social groups. People sculpt their bodies and try to get rid of fat as they modify their eating habits (fearing high cholesterol and fatness), and increase the energy and oxygen capacity of their bodies (e.g., not smoking). The fit, muscular, upright, dynamic body that is exercised almost every day has become the symbol of modernness and even of elitism. Sports turns from a means of competition among talented people to an instrument for individual bodies in competition with time and as a symbol of status. Paul Yonnet suggests that jogging and aerobics provide a summary of Western modernism's affinity with the body, yet they render different meanings. As a sports activity of mostly men, the former stands for a cultural code that embraces long-term endurance and requires slow but long-term, demanding physical effort and the use of limited energy resources. The latter, however, which represents the attempts of women to take part in athletic endeavors and is called "women's boxing" by Paul Yonnet, attempts to reform the female body and to protect its fitness. Both of these activities target the preservation of the body's uprightedness against time, aging, and formlessness.[11]

The principles of equality and of visibility, which are embraced by Western modernism, penetrated the realm of the body and subverted the established hierarchy of ages through their operations against time and aging. The aesthetic of youth is witnessed at the level of clothes as well as of lifestyle; sportswear and stretch clothes have become popular as an expression of muscular, flexible, and fit bodies. Along with the profanation process, the body increasingly undergoes human control and clings to the "present" time.

The Islamic body, which resists secularization, however, shows its difference with Western modernism using different semantics. The hierarchy of genders and ages are marked out clearly, and differences are accentuated; furthermore, fine gestures of the body are subject to discipline and to religious knowledge. The soul, which is controlled by means of the body itself, is purified for the other world. The hierarchy of ages is strictly preserved, and each period in one's lifetime—such as virginity, marriage, bearing of children—is important in determining one's social position and mapping out his or her behavior. The distinction between the sexes is also hierarchic, the ban on the visibility of women reinforcing the hegemony of men. The privilege assigned to men of "looking" and "seeing" provides sexual privileges to them by objectifying the female body.[12] Although women assume that they are not objects thanks to their veils, in fact the very act of veiling per se expresses the visual privilege of men.

Hence, when the veiling of women is claimed as the symbol of Islamic movements, what is actually being acted out is the intersection of political ideology and the power relations between the sexes. With the act of veiling women perform a political statement against Western modernism, yet at the same time they seem to accept the male domination that rests their own invisibility and their confinement to the private sphere. Nevertheless, this could well be an extension of traditionalism itself, since it consists of certain essentialist definitions.[13] Macleod has pointed out that the veiling of Islamic women, on the one hand, "confirms" their traditional female roles, while, since it represents political opposition, it also signifies an "accommodating protest," on the other.[14]

The veil designates good manners and trancendence. The Islamic body shows itself against the deified Western one with its rhythmic quality (veiling, ablution, worshiping, praying), its obedience and submission to the sacred orders. It is thus the female body that emerges as the most visible symbol of distinction from Western civilization. Along with the politicization of Islam, the female body uncovers the dark side of modernism with the act of veiling. In a sense the present rise of Islamic movements corresponds to the return of Muslim social actors to the history from which they were expelled when the idea for society was progress as defined by the Western world.

Islamic Identity and Social Participation

Explanatory frameworks constructed on the basis of dualities such as traditional/modern, Islam/the West, and reactionary/progressivist are not useful in the analysis of hybrid and complex phenomena. Thus, the exposition of Islamic movements as anti-Westernist and representative of traditionalism and/or reactionism is futile. It must also be kept in mind that Western modernism itself has undergone an evolutionary process. Hence, when the criticisms based on the damaging impact of the Age of Enlightenment's passion for "progress" are taken into consideration, our approach to modernity as well as the Islamic phenomena will inevitably be widened.

The principle of equality has acted as the dynamo in the operation of democratic societies since the birth of the industrial societies. The more the principle of equality is recognized at the level of social imagination, the more it accelerates the operations of social practice. The social movements that target the overthrow of the inequality that exists between the races, classes, nations, and, finally, genders, and the politics produced by these movements provide indicators for the historical evolution that the democratic societies followed. These societies today set out the *principle of difference* against the *principle of equality*, with the criticism that the latter homogenizes and represses democratizing, particular local and national cultures. Hence, postmodern culture speaks for local cultures, plurality, differences, and the free flow of relativism and its communication.

As the cultural mode of the communication age, postmodernism gives credit to localism rather than universalism, plurality of values and practices instead of the homogenizing values of industrial culture. In the meantime different identities and local experiences converge by means of communication within the process of globalization. Yet it is necessary to beware of falling into the trap of neotraditionalism, which may easily emerge as a consequence of the disparity between the search for difference and the principle of equality. The passion for equality marked universalism onto human experiences and freed them from being a part of a relativistic, split mosaic. It also eliminated the transcendence of the essentialist definitions that provide a basis for differences between the races, genders, and nations. The humanist and rationalist outlooks extended to more and more spheres of human experience secularization and exalted the power of the human will over social life.

The participation of women as subjects in social life became possible with the criticism of essentialist definitions and the struggle for equality in opportunity, occupation, and rights between men and women. The feminist movement, on the one hand, made progress in the society, with the assistance of the equality principle, and, on the other hand, represented the search for identity, which sprang from the 1960s counterculture tradition. Thus, it may be argued that the women's movement operated on a twofold basis: as an action for equality, enabling women to participate in industrial society, and as a critical action, resisting the suppression of the female identity. It is within this context that the danger lies of falling into conservative responses to essentialist definitions (the so-called legitimate grounds of human existence), once the search for difference and identity becomes estranged from the principle of equality.

The Islamist movement and Islamic women in particular look for a basis for social action along with a tolerance for differences and separate identities. This search is an attempt to resurrect Islamic culture, and people themselves, in the collective memory as well as social life and to counter the homogenizing and dismissive processes of the Westernist transformation to civilization.

Hence, the Islamic movement stands not far from Western social movements that flourished within the countercultural traditions, such as with the slogan of Black Is Beautiful, in itself a critique of "assimilation" (i.e., into white culture) and which spoke of repressed identity.[15] Similarly, Islamic identity functions as a lever in the social process. Behind the political movements lie the dynamics of social participation.[16] Thus, Islam does not stand against modernity; rather, it acts as a compass of life and as a means of management with modern society. Drawing attention to social participation and current dynamics, "in a culture where elites stand far from the people, individuals will prefer to be the 'folk elites' and "where the opportunities provided after education are all closed, people will prefer Qur'an courses," writes Mardin.[17] The author further argues that religion will influence the management of everyday life, a task that was abandoned by grand ideologies and Kemalist modernization, and it will also function as a "social guide," providing a map that deciphers appropriate behavior codes in the society.[18] It defines "good" and "bad," orients itself toward the inner world, regulates the everyday life, determines the syntax of intersex and interpersonal relations.

As Durkheim has noted, religion constructs a web of interpersonal relations and social solidarity by means of its rituals and collectively shared feelings. For Durkheim the social bond is an outcome of the profane "division of labor" as much as a product of sacred "belief" and companionship. Thus, it is possible to reason that the Islamist movements recreate the social bond lost as a consequence of modernization and reconstitute a "lost community" at the level of social imagination. Benedict Anderson, who defines nationalism as an "imagined community" in which deep and horizontal relations among people who have never encountered one another are maintained, prefers to approach the question of nationalism at the levels of "religion" and "blood relations" rather than as political ideology.[19] In this vein it seems reasonable to conclude that the Islamic movements constitute the "imagined communities" and, furthermore, that the religion of Islam appears as mortar in a new nationalism that functions in opposition to Kemalism which aims to be independent of the local patterns embodied in the Islamic religion.[20]

At the same time, however, it is reasonable to acknowledge the fact that the political ideologies and searches for new power are constantly tested by social practice. When the ways "contemporary Islamic discourse"[21] transforms its political practices and individual strategies by social actors are examined, it becomes clear that power relations between the sexes intersect with politics. Islam, which promotes horizontal relations between individuals, brotherhood, as well as imagined communitarian relations, is independent of the power relations between the sexes. The veiling of women symbolizes the Islamic organizations and constitutes a base for the politicization of Islam and for the perpetuation of the segregation between the sexes, meaning the confinement of women to the *mahrem*, the domestic sphere. Paradoxically, the more Islamic women enter the public sphere via political movements, the more influential they become in initiating an irreversible process within the Islamic movement, when they "question" the private sphere. When Islamic women point to their "individual" life strategies instead of their "collective" political identities as their top priority and when they move their "inner worlds," the realm of prohibitions, to the "outer worlds," they not only constitute their own identities but also transform existing relations between women and men. Speculations that center on their "subordination to men" or "their manipulation by reactionaries" or their passive roles within the Islamic movement remain incomplete in deciphering the meanings embedded within present practices.

Inspired by Michel Foucault, we can hope that when power relations are perceived as a form of constant production of reality instead of a repressive power apparatus based upon the hegemony of men, then our approach to the connections between the Islamic movement and the role of women will focus upon everyday practices and thus will be enriched. Islamic women who have used the "opportunity realm"[22] granted to women by Kemalism have rejected Islamic prohibitions and have subverted the established relations between men and women in the *mahrem* sphere as well as increased their own participation in the public realm. As it is different from Kemalist feminism, it is troubling for these women to speak out about their demands for participation in the social life, since it requires subversion of the prevalent gender relations embedded in the private sphere. Following the fathers and sons of the Tanzimat Period, and progressive fathers and their "ideal daughters" of the Period of Kemalist Reforms (and feminist women who disowned the inheritance of their mothers), gender relations between women and men have once again been brought into the light as an outcome of the Islamic movement. Gender relations will be the key determinant to whether the Islamist movements evolve toward pluralism, which recognizes individual rights and civil society, or to the terrain of countersociety, which produces totalitarian tendencies.

It seems that certain challenges remain for Turkish society for years to come: whether it will be possible for Turks to refasten the broken chains between our past and present time; between local values, local patterns, and elitist cultural products; in short, between the traditionalism and modernity in our memories and in our social reality—whether modernity (as an invention of traditions) will be accomplished and whether our present disharmony with modernity will be eliminated.

Notes

1. The terms *Islamic movements* and *radical Islamism* are used interchangeably in this text, designating the contemporary Islamic movements as a collective action whose ideology was shaped during the late 1970s by Islamist thinkers all over the Muslim world (such as Abu-l Maudoodi in India, Sayyid Qutb in Egypt, Ali Shariati in Iran, and Ali Bulaç in Turkey) and by the Iranian Revolution. The term *radicalism* is used in the sense that there is a return to the origins, to the fundamentals of Islam, to address a critique to Western modernity on the one hand and a desire to realize a systemic change, to create an Islamic society, on the other. The terms *Islamic* and *Islamism* are not differentiated, although the latter term refers to the project of transforming society through political and social empowerment and the former to Muslim culture and religion in general.

2. The contemporary form of Islamist veiling is a head scarf that completely covers the hair, throat, and upper part of the chest and a long, loose-fitting gown in a discreet color that reaches to the heels.

3. The categories of East and West, rather than pointing to fixed geographical entities, refer to cultural representations that are not independent from the relations of domination between developed Western countries and the non-Western ones (labeled differently according to ideological epochs, such as Eastern, Third World, and recently Islamic). As the East was an integral part in the development of Western identity, similarly the West has been woven into the history making of the East. For the problematization of these categories, see Edward Said, *Orientalism* (New York: Pantheon, 1978).

4. Micaela di Leonardo, ed., *Gender at the Crossroads of Knowledge: Feminist Anthropology in the Postmodern Era* (Berkeley: University of California Press, 1991), 30–31.

5. C. Wright Mills, *The Sociological Imagination* (London: Penguin Books, 1971).

6. For instance, as *Le Monde* indicate, France witnessed a very passionate "juridical, political and quasi-philosophical dispute" around the rights of female Muslim students covering their heads in French high schools, often referred to in the media as *"l'affaire du foulard."* Recently, legislation ("la circulaire Bayrou," 20 September 1994) prohibited the utilization of all "ostentatious

signs" in high schools. For the debate on "La France et l'Islam," see *Le Monde*, 13 October 1994.

7. For an analysis of the differentiation between traditional, pious and Islamist styles and the symbolic functions of covering in Egypt, see Andrea B. Rugh, *Reveal and Conceal: Dress in Contemporary Egypt* (Syracuse: Syracuse University Press, 1986); and Sherifa Zuhur, *Revealing Reveiling: Islamist Gender Ideology in Contemporary Egypt* (New York: State University of New York Press, 1992).

8. Pierre Bourdieu, *La Distinction: critique sociale du jugement* (Paris: Editions du Minuit, 1979) (pub. in English as *Distinction* [Cambridge, Mass.: Harvard University Press, 1984]).

9. For the analysis of the events and the terms of this debate, see Emelie A. Olson, "Muslim Identity and Secularism in Contemporary Turkey: The Headscarf Dispute," Anthropological Quarterly 58, no. 6 (Oct. 1985).

10. Islamists themselves do not use the word *turban* and are critical of this label, preferring to use *tessettür*, that is, covering of women, or in modern Turkish *başörtüsü* (headscarf).

11. For a criticism of culturalist essentialism and its relation to postmodernism, see Aziz Al-Azmeh, *Islams and Modernities* (London: Verso, 1993).

12. Zygmunt Bauman, *Legislators and Interpreters: On Modernity, Post-Modernity and Intellectuals* (Ithaca, N.Y.: Cornell University Press, 1987).

13. The Turkish word *çağdaş* (contemporary) used synonymously with *modern*, is conceptualized more in terms of the "coming future," progress; it does not invoke the "present" time. It is interesting to note that the concepts "modernity" and modernism" have been widely used in Turkish for a decade because of Turkish intellectuals' interest in the postmodern debate. But its use as such differentiates more and more the "modern" from the "West."

14. Alain Touraine, *Production de la société* (Paris: Editions du Seuil, 1973) pub. in English as *The Self-Production of Society*, trans. Derek Coltman [Chicago: The University of Chicago Press, 1977]).

15. Alain Touraine, *La Voix et le regard* (Paris: Editions du Seuil, Paris, 1978) (pub. as *The Voice and the Eye: An Analysis of Social Movement* [Cambridge: Cambridge University Press, 1981]). Touraine speaks of historicity as the creation of a historical experience and not of a position in historical evolution. He defines historicity as "the set of cultural models a society uses to produce its norms in the domains of knowledge, production, and ethics," Alain Touraine, *Critique of Modernity* (Cambridge: Blackwell, 1995), 368–69.

16. Michel Foucault, *L'Usage des plaisirs*, vol. 2: *Histoire de la sexualité* (Paris: Editions Gallimard, 1984). (pub. as *The History of Sexuality*, vol. 1, trans. Robert Hurley [New York: Vintage Books, 1990]).

17. Somers and Gibson argue forcefully for "joining narrative to identity," a condition, according to the authors, of introducing "time, space, and analytic relationality" and thereby circumventing "essentialist" approaches to identity. For the methodological implications of the concept of narrative for the social theory of action, see Margaret G. Somers and Gloria D. Gibson, "Reclaiming the Epistemological 'Other': Narrative and the Social Constitution of Identity," in

Social Theory and the Politics of Identity, ed. Craig Calhoun (Cambridge, Mass.: Blackwell, 1994), 65 and 37–90.

18. For a detailed discussion of these principles, see Touraine, *La Voix.* The author has participated with Alain Touraine in studying the new social movements, particularly the feminist movement, in France. Apart from studying Islamist veiled women, she has also conducted research according to the principles of sociological intervention on leftist engineers in Turkey. The discussion of sociological intervention accounts for her own interpretation of the method in relation to the research conducted on Islamist women.

19. Mustafa Kemal Pasha (1881–1938), the Ottoman general who led the War of Independence (1919–1922), was given the name Atatürk (father of Turks) when he established the Republic of Turkey in 1923. Kemalism refers to his modernist and secularist ideology that has continued to influence Turkish society to this day. Kemalist reforms refer to the transition from the multiethnic Ottoman Empire to the foundation of a secular republican nation-state (1923). The abolition of the Caliphate (1924), the abolition of Sharia, and the adoption of the Swiss civil code (1926), and the abandonment of the Arabic script, replacing it with the Latin alphabet (1928), were among the Kemalist reforms. See Bernard Lewis, *The Emergence of Modern Turkey* (London: Oxford University Press, 1968).

20. Daryush Shayegan, *Le Regard mutilé* (Paris: Albin Michel, 1989).

21. Norbert Elias, *The History of Manners: The Civilizing Process,* vol. 1 (New York: Pantheon, 1978).

22. Ibid., 5.

23. Ibid., 50.

24. There is abundant recent research in different contexts on the centrality of the "woman question," ranging from investigations of modernization, colonialism, and Islamism to the gendered nature of power relations. See Leila Ahmed, *Women and Gender in Islam* (New Haven: Yale University Press, 1992). In the Iranian context the "women's issue" has held a privileged position in the writings of the ideologues of the constitutional revolutionary period (1905–11); see, for instance, Farzaneh Milani, *Veils and Words: The Emerging Voices of Iranian Women Writers* (Syracuse: Syracuse University Press, 1992); Deniz Kandiyoti, ed., *Women, Islam and the State* (Philadelphia: Temple University Press, 1991), 48–76.

25. For a discussion on the Islamic worldview, encompassing the Koran, its interpretations and the images of the Prophet's wives as models for emulation (sources of *sunna*) defining female righteousness based on segregation and modesty, see Barbara F. Stowasser, *Women in the Qur'an, Traditions, and Interpretation* (Oxford: Oxford University Press, 1994). For a discussion of the cultural code of honor and modesty from an anthropological point of view, see Lila Abu-Lughod, *Veiled Sentiments: Honor and Poetry in a Bedouin Society* (Berkeley: University of California Press, 1986).

26. The Kemalist paradigm involves the ideological and intellectual premises of Turkish modernity, which can be summarized as the master-narrative of secularism, republicanism, and gender equality.

27. I am therefore not in agreement with the prevalent Turkish "feminist" reading of the relation between Kemalism and women's rights, highlighting the "given" and not "taken" nature of women's rights, the absent or limited agency on the part of women, and the predominance of patriarchal nationalism. These ready-made formulations of the Western feminist discourse fall short, in my view, as explanations of the particular relationships between Kemalism and women in Turkey.

28. This explains why, in contemporary Turkey, the violation of women's rights and secularism hurts the feelings of the elite more than does the violation of human rights and democracy.

29. Sarah Graham-Brown, *Images of Women: The Portrayal of Women in Photography of the Middle East, 1860–1950* (New York: Columbia University Press, 1988).

30. For a critique of the superficial Westernization of Turkish novels and their male characters, see Şerif Mardin, "Super Westernization in the Ottoman Empire in the Last Quarter of the Nineteenth Century," in *Turkey: Geographic and Social Perspectives,* ed. P. Benedict et al. (Leiden: E. J. Brill, 1974).

31. Milani, *Veils and Words,* 238.

32. It is to be observed that *alaturka* is still used currently in the everyday language of Turkish elites, with a negative connotation—although in recent years there is an appreciation, a sort of nostalgic romantic feeling, for Ottoman and early Turkish taste, cooking, furniture, etc.

33. Milani, *Veils and Words.*

34. For the elaboration and use of the concept of *habitus* in relation to lifestyles, see Bourdieu, *La Distinction,* 189–248.

35. In terms of historical classification and political experience, the Democrat Party legacy, which characterized the transition to political pluralism in Turkey in 1946, is of crucial importance. The Democrat Party, considered by state elites to be too liberal on religious and economic issues, gave voice to those segments of society that were not part of the bureaucratic Kemalist state; it therefore created political mediation, a buffer between the state and society. We can even claim that, instead of Turkey's secularism, which has been imitated to a certain extent in a majority of Muslim countries, it is the Democrat Party legacy that defines Turkish "specificity." I omit the Democrat Party legacy argument here because I think that rather than creating a new intellectual legacy, it provided a political representation of Muslim identity.

36. Calhoun, *Social Theory.*

37. Touraine, *The Voice and the Eye* (trans. from French, *La Voix et le regard* [Paris: Editions Seuil, 1978]).

38. Alexis de Tocqueville, *De la démocratie en Amérique,* (Paris: Garnier-Flammarion, 1981), with preface by François Furet, 1:32–35.

39. Anthony Giddens, *Modernity and Self-Identity: Self and Society in the Late Modern Age* (Palo Alto, Calif.: Stanford University Press, 1991), 80–81.

40. The notion of the "Islamic self" is not appropriate, in the sense in which *self* implies secularism and separation from the community. But this ambiguity is helpful precisely in understanding how community is recon-

structed and reinterpreted through Islamism and the Muslim self. The politicization of religion thus paradoxically engenders self-reflexivity on the Islamic self.

41. Foucault, *History of Sexuality*, 1:61.

42. C. A. O Van Nieuwenhuijze, *The Lifestyles of Islam* (Leiden: E. J. Brill, 1985), 144.

43. Milani argues that the absence in Persian literature of autobiography as a literary genre demonstrates the "reluctance to talk publicly and freely about the self," a condition confined not only to women, who are "privatized," but also to men, who are expected to be "self-contained." See Milani, *Veils and Words*, 201–2.

44. Here I employ Anderson's analysis of nationalism in the context of Islamism. See Benedict Anderson, *Imagined Communities: Reflections on the Origin and Spread of Nationalism* (Thetford: Thetford Press, 1983).

45. Durkheim long ago pointed out that the two distinct realms—the sacred and profane—are both indispensable for the establishment and reproduction of social ties.

46. Nazih Ayubi, *Political Islam: Religion and Politics in the Arab World* (London and New York: Routledge, 1991), 63.

47. Charles Taylor, *Multiculturalism: Examining the Politics of Recognition*, ed. and intro. Amy Gutman (Princeton: Princeton University Press, 1994).

48. I was hence literally accused of being an "anti-Republican, neo-Ottomanist, ex-communist, neoliberal, fundamentalist, and (Kurdish) separatist" by a female author in a highly critical review of my book and of being highly committed to the master-narrative of nationalism, secularism, and feminism. See Erendiz Atasü, "Postmodern bir aldanış," *Cumhuriyet Kitap* (Literary Supplement of Daily Cumhuriyet), 24 November 1994, 6.

49. It was published in France under the title *Musulmanes et modernes: voile et civilisation en Turquie* (Paris: Editions de la Découverte, 1993).

50. The most elaborate and interesting article was written by one of the leading Islamist intellectuals, Ali Bulaç, positioning himself critically and adding the conjunction *and* to the title *Modern Mahrem* in order to refute the intersection between the two distinct conceptions of social organization, self and civilization, which he conceived in more of a monodirectional sense, as a "modernization of Islam" therefore as a trivialization of it by the forces of modernity and commodity logic. We continue our discussion in public debates and in periodicals. See Ali Bulaç, "Modern ve Mahrem," *Birikim*, no. 33 (January 1992). It is also interesting to note that Islamist intellectual Bulaç published this article in a leftist periodical.

CHAPTER 2

1. The letter Princess Seniha wrote to Madame Simone de la Cherté is dated 30 December 1910. See Claude Farrère, *Türklerin Manevi Gücü* (Istanbul: Tercüman 1001 Temel Eser), 97 (first edition pub. as *Extraordinaire aventure*

d'Ahmet Pacha Djemaleddine [Paris: Ernest Flammarion, 1921]). Seniha was the daughter of Sultan Abdülmechid and Nalandil Hanım and the mother of Prince Sabahattin. See Pars Tuğlacı, *Osmanlı Saray Kadınları* (Istanbul: Cem Yayınevi, 1985).

2. Edward Said, *Orientalism* (New York: Pantheon, 1978).

3. Ibid.

4. H. Desmet-Gregoire, "De la perception d'une femme ottomane à celle des femmes Ottomanes: le récit de voyage d'une européenne du XIXe siècle. La princesse de Belgiojoso,"*Contributions à l'histoire économique et sociale de l'Empire Ottomane* (Louvain: Peeters, 1983), 439.

5. The theories of the social sciences generally refer to these societies in the framework of "underdevelopment," "backwardness," "the Third World," or as on the "peripheries of the world economic system," with the aim of explaining relationships of dependency and of exploitation in economic terms. The concept of weak historicity, however, takes the paradigm of modernity into account as a social practice. It is primarily concerned with the production of modernity, which is assumed to be embedded in the nature and structure as well as in the practice of social relations. It aims to situate weak historicity in ontological narratives, social agency, and ideological representations of actors. In sum this concept aspires to provide an outlook for social practices of societies that could not produce their own history of modernity on the strength of their intrinsic and structural inventories.

6. Daryush Shayegan, *Le Regard mutilé* (Paris: Albin Michel, 1989).

7. Hichem Djait, "Dimensions de l'orientalisme islamisant," *Le Mal de voir* (Paris: Union Generale d'Editions), 259.

8. For an analysis of the initial encounter of Turkish society with the Western world, see Fatma Müge Göçek, *East Encounters West: France and the Ottoman Empire in the Eighteenth Century* (New York: Oxford University Press, 1987).

9. For a detailed account of this issue, see Ismail Kara, *Türkiye'de Islamcılık Düsüncesi* (Istanbul: Risale Yayınları, 1986), 1:xv.

10. Nora Şeni in her article, which particularly focuses on the relationship between the female body and political power (the state), displays how the Ottoman state regulated the clothes worn by women as well as by minorities in the public arena and the way the female body reflected state authority symbolically in urban settlements. See Nora Şeni, "Ville Ottomane et représentations du corps feminin," *Les Temps Modernes* (Turkey) (July-August 1984), 66–95.

11. Niyazi Berkes, *Türkiye'de Çağdaşlaşma* (Ankara: Bilgi Yayınevı, 1973), 328–29 (pub. as *The Development of Secularism in Turkey* [Montréal: McGill University Press], 328–29). Berkes argues that the issue of the liberation of women was touched on by various authors including Ahmed Mithad, Şinasi, and Namık Kemal, although the discussions on women around the two conflicting views were initiated with a series by Mahmut Esad Efendi.

12. Ibid., 329.

13. Ibid., 329.

14. Ibid., 329.

15. Hilmi Ziya Ülken, *Türkiye'de Çağdaş Düşünce Tarihi* (1966; reprint, Istanbul: Ülken Yayınları, 1979), 198.

16. Berkes, *Türkiye'de Çağdaşlaşma*, 336.

17. Özer Özankaya, "Laiklik öncesi dönemde Semseddin Sami'nin aile düzenine iliskin görüsleri," *Türkiye'de Ailenin Değişimi* (Türk Sosyal Bilimler Derneği, 1984), 123–24.

18. Ibid., 123.

19. Ibid., 126–28.

20. For an elaborate account of this controversy, see Muhaddere Taşçıoğlu, *Türk Osmanlı Cemiyetinde Kadının Sosyal Konumu ve Kadın Kıyafetleri* (Ankara: Akın Matbaası, 1958), 31–34.

21. For Ekrem Işın, the mansion education, which gave rise to the proliferation of intellectual women in society, is an adaptation of the classical *harem* educational system of the Ottoman courts to the modernization attempts of the Tanzimat Period. Ekrem Işın, "Tanzimat, kadın ve gündelik hayat," *Tarih ve Toplum* 9, no. 51, (1988): 150–55.

22. Berkes, *Türkiye'de Çağdaşlaşma*, 267.

23. For M. A. Kılıçbay the Tanzimat acts as an attempt to return to the lost Golden Age. Cited in Jale Parla, *Babalar ve Oğullar: Tanzimat Romanının Epistemolojik Temelleri* (Istanbul:İletişim Yayınları, 1990), 11. It is stated in the article of Ekrem Işın, too, that the idea of the Golden Age predominates in the writings of a leading aesthete, Cenab Şehabeddin (Işın, "Tanzimat," 27).

24. For a depiction of the predominance of the "Islamic epistemology" in the writings of these authors, see Parla, *Babalar ve Oğullar*.

25. Ibid., 11–12.

26. Ibid., 16–17.

27. Ibid., 17–18.

28. Ibid., 17.

29. Ibid., 69.

30. Mehmet O. Alkan, "Tanzimat'tan sonra kadının hukuksal statüsü," *Toplum ve Bilim*, no. 50 (Summer 1990): 85–95.

31. Ibid., 88.

32. Işın, "Tanzimat," 27.

33. Tarık Zafer Tunaya, *Türkiye'nin Siyasi Hayatında Batılılaşma Hareketleri* (Istanbul: Yedigün Matbaası, 1960), 77. For the distinct approaches of these intellectual outlooks toward women, see B. Caporal, *Kemalizmde ve Kemalizm Sonrasında Türk Kadını* (Ankara: İş Bankası Kültür Yayınları, 1982), 78. The Westernist outlook is expressed particularly in the magazine *Içtihat*, the Islamic one in the magazines *Volkan, Sırati Müstakim, Sebilürresad,* and *Beyanülhak.* The Turkist outlook is to be found in the publications *Türk Yurdu* and *Yeni Nesil.*

34. An interview with İsmail Kara (Sefa Kaplan), *Nokta*, 31 December 1989.

35. Berkes, *Türkiye'de Çağdaşlaşma*, 337–38.

36. Abdullah Cevdet, "Ictihat," no. 89; 1329, cited in B. Caporal, op. cit., 56.

37. Ibid., 470.

38. Ibid., 338

39. Berkes notices that the school of neo-Westernism, witnessed especially

in the literary works of the period, is generally referred to as "decadent," for it rejects tradition. Ahmet Mithat used the Arabic word *dehri* (contemporaries, uprooted) for this movement. In fact, the word *dehri* is generally used to mean offenders of morality (ibid., 334–39).

40. T. Taşkıran, *Cumhuriyet'in 50. Yılında Türk Kadın Hakları* (Başbakanlık Basımevi: Başbakanlık Kültür Müsteşarlığı, 1973), 49.

41. Salahaddin Asım, *Türk Kadınlığının Tereddisi yahud Karılaşmak* (new edition, *Osmanlıda Kadınlığın Durumu*) (Istanbul: Arba Yayınları, 1989).

42. Ülken, *Türkiye'de Çağdaş*, 395.

43. Asım, 22.

44. Ibid., 27–32.

45. Celal Nuri İleri, *Kadınlarımız*; cited in Taşkıran, *Cumhuriyet'in 50*, 60.

46. Halil Hamit, *İslamiyette Feminizm yahut Alem-i Nisvanda Musava-i Tamme: Kadınlık Aleminde Tam Eşitlik*; cited in Taşkıran, *Cumhuriyet'in 50*, 53.

47. Said Halim Paşa, *Buhranlarımız* (1919; reprint, Instanbul: Tercüman 1001 Eser), 136.

48. Ibid., 142, 143, 145.

49. Ibid., 149.

50. From an article by İskipli Mehmed Atif on imitations of the West and of civilization, in Kara, *Türkiye'de İslamcılık Düsüncesi*, 1:253.

51. From an article by Musa Kazim on "Liberty, Equality, and Women's Rights" in Kara, *Türkiye'de İslamcılık Düsüncesi*, 1:52.

52. Ibid., 54.

53. Ibid.

54. T. Zafer Tunaya, *İslamcılık Cereyanı* (Istanbul: 1962), 101.

55. Caporal, *Kemalizmde*, 83.

56. Ibid., 84.

57. Tunaya, *İslamcılık Cereyanı*, 84.

58. Ibid., 86.

59. Taha Parla, *Ziya Gökalp: Kemalizm ve Türkiye'de Korporatizm* (Istanbul: İletişim Yayınları, 1989), 33.

60. Ziya Gökalp, *Türkçülügün Esasları: Garba Doğru* (Istanbul: Milli Egitim Basımevi, 1976), 48.

61. "Asrı aile ve Milli Aile" (*Yeni Mecmua* [1917]), Ziya Gökalp, *Turkish Nationalism and Western Civilization*, ed. and trans. N. Berkes (London: George Allen and Unwin, 1959), 252.

62. Ibid., 158–64.

63. Caporal, *Kemalizmde*, 97.

64. Gökalp, *Turkish Nationalism*, 163–64.

65. Ibid., 163.

66. See Tasçıoğlu, *Türk*; Caporal, *Kemalizmde*, 141–51; and Şeni, *Ville Ottomane*.

67. Z. Toprak, "*Politics, Women and Family during the II. Constitutional Period*" (Paper presented at the Turkish Family and Domestic Organization Symposium, New York, 23–25 April 1986).

68. Z. Toprak, "Kadınlar Halk Fırkası," *Tarih ve Toplum* 9, no. 51 (1988): 30–31.

69. Caporal, *Kemalizde,* 150.

70. Ibid., 146–49.

71. M. Şehmuz Güzel, "1908 Kadınları," *Tarih ve Toplum* 2, no. 7 (1984): 6–12.

72. Ibid.

73. J. Melia, *Mustafa Kemal ou la rénovation de la Turquie* (Paris, 1929); cited in Caporal, *Kemalizde,* 147–48.

74. Ibid.

75. C. Farrère, I. Letter, 30 December 1910, 95.

76. Ibid., V. Letter, 28 July 1911, 121.

77. Ibid., VI. Letter, 10 August 1912, 129.

78. Ibid., V. Letter, 28 July 1911, 124.

79. D. Shayegan, *Le regard mutilé,* 106.

80. Kara, *Türkiye'de,* xvi-vii.

81. Ibid., xxiv-v.

82. Alexis de Tocqueville, *De la Démocratie en Amerique I* (Paris: Garnier-Flammarion, 1981), 32–33.

83. There exist two dimensions to the feminist movement: one based on the principle of equality, the other on the principle of difference. Here I am referring to the former. Along with the movement against the industrial cultural model, the issues of identity and difference became more crucial in the feminist movement.

84. Michel Foucault, *The History of Sexuality,* vol. 1 (London: Allen Lane, 1979).

85. Ibid.

86. Ismail Hakkı Izmirli, "Islamda Kadin Hakları," in Kara, *Türkiye'de,* 112–19.

87. Zafer Toprak, "Kadın askerler ve Milli Aile," *Tarih ve Toplum* 9, no. 51 (1988): 34–38.

88. Zafer Toprak, "Meşrutiyet yıllarında kadınlara dair söylenmiş sözler," *Tarih ve Toplum* 9, no. 51 (1988): 46.

89. Safa, *Türk İnkılabına Bakışlar,* 55.

90. Ibid., 51–52.

91. Taner Timur, *Osmanlı Kimliği* (Istanbul: Hil Yayınları, 1986), 13.

92. Safa, *Türk İnkılabına Bakışlar,* 34.

93. Berkes, *Türkiye'de Çağdaşlaşma,* 334.

94. Ibid.

95. Safa, *Türk İnkılabına Bakışlar,* 35.

96. Asım, 147–52.

97. Şerif Mardin, *Türk,* 98.

98. Gökalp, Türkçülüğün, 7, 60.

99. Gökalp, *Limmi ve Malta Mektupları,* ed. F. A. Tansel (Ankara: Türk Tarih Kurumu Yayınları, 1965), 47.

100. Zafer Toprak, "Kadın askerler ve Milli Aile," and "Politics, Women and Family during the II. Constitutional Period," ibid.

101. Halide Edip Adıvar, *Yeni Turan,* 5th ed. (1912; reprint, Istanbul: Atlas Kitabevi, 1982), 17, 18, 28.

CHAPTER 3

1. Depending upon their demographic analyses, Duben and Behar refer to the structural changes of the Turkish family (especially between the years 1920 and 1930) in reference to the "civilizational shift." Alan Duben and Cem Behar, *Istanbul Households: Marriage, Family and Fertility, 1880–1940* (Cambridge: Cambridge University Press, 1991).

2. Ziya Gökalp, *Türkçülüğün Esasları: Kültür Bakanlığı Yayınları* (Istanbul: Milli Eğitim Basımevi, 1976), 50.

3. Peyami Safa, *Türk Inkilabına Bakışlar* (1938; reprint, Kanaat Kitabevi: Ankara Kütüphanesi Tarih Serisi, 1959), 7.

4. Ahmet Hamdi Tanpınar, *Yaşadığım Gibi,* (Istanbul: Dergah Yayınları, n.d.), 24–35.

5. Paul Gentizon, *Mustapha Kemal ou L'Orient en marche,* ed. Bossard (Paris, 1929), 62.

6. P. Dumont, *Mustafa Kemal* (Paris: Complexe, 1983), 156.

7. N. Elias, *La Civilization des moeurs* (Paris: Calmann Levy, 1973) (first pub. in German, 1969).

8. Ibid., 27–51.

9. Safa, *Türk Inkilabına Bakışlar,* 90.

10. Nora Şeni, "19. Yüzyıl Sonu Istanbul Basınında Moda ve Kadın Kıyafetleri," *Kadın Bakış Açısından 1980'ler Türkiye'sinde Kadın,* ed. Şirin Tekeli (Istanbul: Iletişim Yayınları, 1990), 62.

11. Because of the popularity of starched shirts and neckties, the verse "The frock coat suits my clerk" was replaced with "The starched shirt suits my clerk" in the Katibim song. See Cevdet Kudret, "Alafranga dedikleri," *Tarih ve Toplum* 1, no. 4 (1984): 267-68.

12. La Baronne D. de Fontmagne, *Eski Istanbul Yaşayışı* (Istanbul: Kervan Yayınları, 1977); cited in Nuray Mert, *A Study on the Change of Clothing Habits* (Thesis, Department of History, Bogaziçi University, 1983), 4.

13. Cevdet Kudret, "Alafranga dedikleri," *Tarih ve Toplum* 1, no. 4 (1984): 267-71.

14. Mahmut Göloğlu, *Devrimler ve Tepkileri* (1924–1930) (Ankara: Başnur Matbaası, 1972), 141.

15. Ibid., 141.

16. Cihan Aktaş, *Kılık, Kıyafet ve İktidar* (Istanbul: Nehir Yayınları, 1989), 1:137–64.

17. Ernest Jackh, *Yükselen Hilal* (Uğur Kitabevi, 1946), 51.

18. P. Gentizon, 167; *Kemalizmde ve Kemalizm Sonrasinda Türk Kadini* (Ankara: İş Bankası Kültür Yayınları, 1982), 651.

19. Tarık Zafer Tunaya, "Milli Rönesans," *Tarih ve Toplum* 5, no. 26 (1986): Page of Atatürk, 117.

20. İdris Küçükömer argues that the bureaucratic class positioned itself against the Easternist Islamic people's front, backed by the union of Janissaries, *ulema,* and tradesmen. As for "the left wing," he mentions Prince Sabahattin, Freedom and Agreement, the Second Group of the League for the Defence of

National Rights at the First Turkish Grand National Assembly, the Progressivist Party, the Liberal Party, the Democratic Party, and the Justice Party. See İdris Küçükömer, *Düzenin Yabancılaşması* (1969; reprint, Istanbul: Alan Yayınlari, 1989).

21. François Georgeon, *Türk Milliyetçiliğinin Kökenleri: Yusuf Akçura* (Ankara: Yurt Yayınları, 1986), 113.

22. The Turkish nationalists published the magazine *Halka Doğru* (Toward the Public) in 1912, which succeeded *Türk Yurdu* (Turkish Fatherland). The identification of the exaltation of the nation and that of the public in fact indicates the organic affinity between the principles of Turkish nationalism and populism. According to François Georgeon, the Ottoman intelligenstia was deeply influenced by Russia, "the homeland of populism." He further states that the idea of Ziya Gökalp, "going to the people," was first introduced by Hüseyinzade Ali in Turkey. See ibid., 90–91.

23. Şirin Tekeli, *Kadınlar ve Toplumsal Hayat* (Istanbul: Birikim, 1982), 210.

24. Şirin Tekeli, "Türkiye'deki kadının siyasi hayattaki yeri," in *Türk Toplumunda Kadın*, ed. N. A. Unat (1979; reprint, Istanbul: Ekin Yayınları, 1982), 380–81.

25. *Atatürk'ün Söylev ve Demeçleri* (The Speeches of Atatürk), *Konya Kadınları ile Konuşma*, 21, March 1923, 147.

26. Muhaddere Taşçıoğlu, *Türk Osmanlı Cemiyetinde Kadının Sosyal Durumu ve Kadın Kıyafetleri* (Ankara: Akin Matbaası, 1958), 74.

27. Ibid., 74.

28. *Hanımlara Mahsus Gazete* (Newspaper of Women), 21 October 1985, cited in Mert, *Study on the Change of Clothing Habits*, 4.

29. Şeni, "19. Yüzyil Sono Istanbul," 48, 57.

30. See Mert, *Study on the Change of Clothing Habits*, 31. In addition, Muhaddere Taşçıoğlu follows a similar argument.

31. Georg Simmel, *Philosophie de la modernité: la femme, la ville, l'individualisme* (Paris: Editions Payot, 1989), 174 (first pub. in German, 1923).

32. Yakup Kadri Karaosmanoğlu, *Ankara* (1934; reprint, Istanbul: İletişim Yayınları, 1987), 96.

33. Simmel, *Philosophie*, 179.

34. Mert, *Study on the Change of Clothing Habits*, 22.

35. Hadiye İzzet, "Moda sevdasını bırakalım," *Kadınlar Dünyası*, 13 May 1329 (26.05.1913); cited in ibid., 22.

36. Karaosmanoğlu, *Ankara*, 129.

37. Ibid., 91.

38. Ibid., 167.

39. Ibid., 109.

40. Halide Edip Adıvar, *Raik'in Annesi* (1912; reprint, Istanbul: Atlas Kitabevi, 1990), 133.

41. Halide Edip Adıvar, *Yeni Turan* (1912; reprint, Istanbul: Atlas Kitabevi, 1990), 17–18.

42. Berna Moran, *Türk Romanına Eleştirel Bir Bakış I* (1983; reprint, Istanbul: İletişim Yayınları, 1990), 119.

43. Inci Enginün, *Halide Edip Adıvar'ın Eserlerinde Doğu ve Batı Meselesi* (Istanbul: Edebiyat Fakültesi Matbaası, 1978), 23.

44. Ayşe Durakbaşa, *The Formation of Kemalist Female Identity: A Historical-Cultural-Perspective* (Thesis, Department of Sociology, Boğaziçi University, 1987), 109.

45. Falih Rıfkı Atay, *Çankaya*; cited in Aktaş, *Kılık*, 156.

46. Ibid.

47. Nora Şeni claims a continuity between Ottoman and Republican Turkey in terms of the control exercised on individuals through the implementation of regulations on clothing and behavior by the state authority. See Şeni, "Ville ottomane et représentation du corps feminin," *Les Temps Modernes* (Turkey), nos. 456–57 (July-August 1984): 83–85.

48. "Osmanlı yaşayışiyla ilgili belgeler-bilgiler: Kadın-I," *Tarih ve Toplum* 1, no. 3 (1984): 192–99.

49. "Osmanlı yaşayışiyla ilgili belgeler-bilgiler: Kadın-II", *Tarih ve Toplum* 1, no. 4 (1984): 296.

50. Fatima Mernissi, *Beyond the Veil* (1985; reprint, Bloomington and Indianapolis: Indiana University Press, 1987), 27–45.

51. Taşçioğlu, *Türk*, 81–82.

52. Louis Beck and Nikki Keddie, eds., *Women in the Muslim World* (Cambridge, Mass.: Harvard University Press, 1978), 27.

53. Berkes, *Türkiye'de Çağdaşlaşma*, 470.

54. The discussions on the civil law are all cited from Caporal's book. See Caporal, *Kemalizmde*, 350–86.

55. Ibid.

56. Ibid.

57. Ibid.

58. Nevertheless, Nermin Abadan-Unat evinced that the civil law does not in fact allow for an absolute principle of equality between spouses in the family (e.g., "the head of the family is the husband," "a woman is not allowed to work without the permission of her husband," "a woman is not allowed to maintain her maiden surname," etc.). See Nermin Abadan-Unat, "Toplumsal değişme ve kadın," in *Türk Toplumunda Kadın*, ed. Nermin Abadan-Unat (Ankara: Türk Sosyal Bilimler Derneği Yayınları, 1982). Today, with pressure from feminist groups, these clauses are waiting to be changed.

59. For the determining role of father-daughter relations on the Kemalist female identity and the "silent agreement," see Durakbaşa, *Formation of Kemalist Female Identity*, 125

60. Ibid.

61. Süreyya Ağaoğlu, *Bir Ömür Böyle Geçti* (Ağaoğlu Yayınları, 1984), 41–42.

62. Durakbaşa, *Formation of Kemalist Female Identity*, 124.

63. Yeşim Arat, *The Patriarchal Paradox: Women Politicians in Turkey* (London and Toronto: Associated University Presses, 1989).

64. Cited in Özer Özankaya, "Şemseddin Sami'nin aile düzenine ilişkin görüşleri," *Türkiye'de Ailenin Değişimi*, 129.

65. Ibid.

66. Caporal, *Kemalizmde,* 386.

67. Deniz Kandiyoti, "Ataerkil örüntüler: Türk toplumunda erkek ege-menliğinin çözümlenmesine yönelik notlar," *Kadın Bakış Açısından 1980'ler Türkiye'sinde Kadın,* 351.

68. Durakbaşa, *Formation of Kemalist Female Identity,* 93–94.

69. Edip, *Yeni Turan,* 28–29.

70. Hilmi Yavuz, *Roman Kavramı ve Türk Romanı* (Ankara: Bilgi Yayınevı, 1977), 156–63.

71. Ibid., 160–61.

72. Ibid., 161–62.

73. Şirin Tekeli, "The Meaning and the Limits of Feminist Ideology in Turkey," *The Study of Women in Turkey: An Anthology,* ed. Ferhunde Özbay (MS, UNESCO and Türk Sosyal Bilimler Derneği, 1986).

74. Ferhunde Özbay, "Development of Studies on Women in Turkey," *Study of Women in Turkey.*

75. Nükhet Sirman, "Feminism in Turkey: A Short History," *New Perspectives on Turkey* 3, no. 1 (Fall 1989): 1–34.

76. Fatmagül Berktay, "Türkiye solunun kadına bakışı: değişen bir şey var mi?" *Kadın Bakış Açısından 1980'ler Türkiye'sinde Kadın,* 289–300; see also Tekeli, *Meaning and Limits,* 191–92.

77. Berktay, *"Türkiye,"* 291.

78. Kandiyoti, *"Ataerkil örüntüler,"* 344.

CHAPTER 4

1. See Marcel Ahano ("Le Politologue et l'hystérique," *CEMOTI,* no. 10 [1990]: 70–71) for the depiction of mass behavior in the Iranian revolution and during the post-Khomeini period.

2. Ibid.

3. Ilhan Arsel, *Şeriat ve Kadın* (Istanbul: Orhanlar Matbaası, 1987); see also Oral Çalışlar, *İslamda Kadın ve Cinsellik* (Istanbul: Afa Yayınları, 1991).

4. Bernard Lewis, "Islamic Political Movements," *Middle East Review* (Summer 1985).

5. A brief background of the research: the necessary preparation for the fieldwork began in the spring of 1987 and took place during August and September of the same year. At the first stage of the fieldwork in-depth interviews were held with the leading figures of the Islamic movement. This was followed by ten in-depth interviews with Islamic female students. Consequently, at the final stage of the fieldwork, four group discussions were organized in which ten to twelve veiled Islamic women participated, representatives of different standpoints within the Islamic movement (from the magazines *Kadın ve Aile* and *Girişim* and the daily *Zaman*); they were mainly university students. The main difficulty was establishing a relationship of trust between the researcher

and participants in the group discussions. The participants constantly expressed their uneasiness at being analyzed by an "outsider" and their fear of "being used for another's own ends." They even hesitated to take part in further research meetings, and two of them left the discussions. Also, at the beginning they objected to my tape-recording the discussions, since they stand in fear of the security forces. They later agreed to the tape recorder when I promised to refer to them by pseudonyms in writing about my research.

The group discussions lasted about three hours, and all of the discussions were tape-recorded and then transcribed. Each of the group discussions consisted of "open" and "closed" meetings. One discussant was invited to each open meeting; a male employee of an Islamic magazine, one of the male leaders of the Islamic movement and his wife, and a feminist were among the invited discussants. The first group discussion was held at the office of an Islamic magazine, while the rest were at a "neutral" place, the Center for Science, Art, and Culture (BILSAK).

6. There exists some other research that depicts similar findings. According to Cihan Aktaş, who studied seventy-five veiled students, the majority of the girls' fathers (thirty-six) were civil sector employees (particularly teachers), while the rest were shopkeepers (thirteen) and tradesmen (eleven). Cihan Aktaş, *Tesettür ve Toplum: Başörtülü Öğrencilerin Toplumsal Kökeni Üzerine Bir İnceleme* (Istanbul: Nehir Yayınları, 1991), 75.

Drawing from nine in-depth interviews with veiled students, Feride Acar, too, pointed out that these students usually live in lower-middle-class districts of the city; their mothers are mostly housewives with elementary school educations, and their fathers are low-ranking state employees, workers, or shopkeepers. See Feride Acar, "Türkiye'de İslamcı Hareket ve kadın," *Kadın Bakış Açısından 1980'ler Türkiye'sinde Kadın*, 77–78.

7. Ibid., 87. According to this research, out of seventy-five students, eighteen of them were supported, and thirty were disapproved by their families; fifteen of them were asked not to veil, at least not at school. It is seen that, first, they were not forced to veil by their families, as it is usually argued, and, second, their families attribute significance to the education of their daughters.

8. Ibid., 44–45.

9. Shils points out the fact that the relationship between center and periphery is not only a geographical one, but, in fact, it refers to the operation of the center on the basis of institutions and system of values. Edward Shils, "Centre and Periphery," *The Logic of Personal Knowledge: Essays Presented to Michael Polanyi*, (London: Routledge and Kegan Paul, 1961), 117–30.

10. Abdelwahab Bouhdiba, *La Sexualité en Islam* (Paris: Quadrige, Press Universitaires de France, 1975), 43–57.

11. Fatima Mernissi, *Le Harem politique* (Paris: Albin Michel, 1987), 119–20.

12. Ibid., 109–10.

13. Ibid., 127–29.

14. Ferit Develioğlu, *Osmanlıda Türkçe Ansiklopedik Lugat* (Ankara: Doğuş Matbaası, 1970).

15. Hatice Tuman, "Çiçekler rahmetle büyür," *Mektup*, no. 31 (August 1987): 27.

16. See Acar, "*Türkiye'de İslamci*, 86. Acar acknowledges the reassurance provided by veiling in the competition taking place among women. In a similar vein Toprak also argues that Islam solves the tension between competing roles with the legitimization of traditional sex roles. Binnaz Toprak, "Türk kadını ve din," in *Türk Toplumunda Kadın*, ed. Nermin Abadan-Unat (Ankara: Türk Sosyal Bilimler Derneği, 1979).

17. Aysel Z. Tozduman, *İslam'da Kadın Hakları: Kadın ve Aile* (Ankara: 1988), 143.

18. For the educational level of the Islamic militants in Egypt, see Saad Eddin İbrahim, "Anatomy of Egypt's Militant Islamic Groups", *International Journal of Middle East Studies* (1980): 423–53. For the Turkish case, see Gencay Şaylan, "Genç Müslümanlar ve İslamcı Hareket," *Cumhuriyet*, 18–23 March 1990.

19. Fadwa El-Guindi, "Veiled Activism: Egyptian Women in the Contemporary Islamic Movement," *Peuples Méditerranéens* 22–23 (1983): 70–90.

20. Cited in Aktaş, *Tesettür ve Toplum*, 77.

21. Daniel Lerner, *The Passing of Traditional Society: Modernizing the Middle East* (New York: The Free Press, 1958).

22. For analyses of Islamic women's magazines, see Acar, *Türkiye'de İslamci*, 73–74; and Yeşim Arat, "Feminizm ve İslam: Kadın ve Aile dergisinin düşündürdükleri," *Kadın Bakış Açısından 1980'ler Türkiye'sinde Kadın*, 94.

23. Aktaş, *Türkiye'de İslamci*, 122.

24. Ibid., 133.

25. Hüseyin Hatemi, *Kadının Çıkış Yolu* (Ankara: Fecr Yayınevi, 1988), 12ff.

26. Germaine Tillion, *Le Harem et les cousins* (Paris: Seuil, 1966), 161–62.

27. Ibid., 161–78.

28. Mernissi, *Le Harem politique*, 238.

29. Ibid., 163.

30. Ibid., 246.

31. Bouhdiba, *La Sexualité*, 144.

32. Ibid.,20.

33. Ibid., 129.

34. Ibid., 144–47.

35. Ibid., 282.

36. For the complementarity of ideology and utopia in every social movement, see Karl Mannheim, *Ideology and Utopia* (New York: Harvest Books, 1936). See also Paul Ricoeur, "L'Histoire comme récit et comme pratique," *Esprit*, no. 6 (June 1981).

37. For a general analysis of the Islamic movements observed in Turkey, see Ruşen Çakır, *Ayet ve Slogan* (Istanbul: Metis Yayınları, 1990).

38. Gilles Kepel, *La Revanche de Dieu* (Paris: Seuil, 1991).

39. Ali Bulaç, *İslam Dünyasında Düşünce Sorunları* (Istanbul: İnsan Yayınları, 1985), 227.

40. Mehmet Metiner, "İsmail Kara ile söyleşi," *Girişim* (May 1987): 12.

41. İsmail Kara, "İslamcılar, mucizeler, bilim ve pozitivizm," *Dergah,* no. 6 (August 1990): 18–19.

42. Çakır, *Ayet ve Slogan* 252, 254.

43. The fact that, in contrast to the experiences of other Muslim countries, the Islamic movement in Turkey follows the intellectual schools of the Western world has attracted the attention of various researchers. The books of Feyerabend, Deleuze and Guattari (*Capitalism and Schizophrenia*), Illich, and Marcuse are very popular among Islamic intellectuals. In his book *Waldo Sen Neden Burada Değilsin?* (Waldo, Why Are You Not Here?) İsmet Özel refers to the American liberationists and those who resist imperialism with citizenship consciousness. Following Heidegger, Avcı in his book *Bombacı Parmenides* elaborates on the originality and totality of every culture, noting the affinity between the prevalent technology and ancient Greek philosophy as well as between the atomic bomb and the poems of Parmenides. Ali Bulaç discusses the theories of postmodernism in his book *Din ve Modernizm* (Religion and Modernism). It is even the case that one Muslim intellectual has said: "If so, Muslims will be the real followers of 1968, the Frankfurt School and antipsychiatry. For instance, certain names like Capra, Illich and Foucault are very much respected and popular among Muslims"; cited in Çakır, *Ayet va Slogan,* 267–68.

44. Necati Polat, "Nabi Avcı ile söyleşi," *Gergadan,* no. 11 (January 1988).

45. This is a citation by one of the leading female representatives of the Muslim Brotherhood in Egypt, who said that "we should have been able to make the first atomic bomb," Avcı acknowledges the complementarity of technics and culture in a statement on Turkish Muslim intellectuals who "somehow know that someone called Parmenides lived and the atomic bomb did not come into existence on its own" (Nabi Avcı, *Bombacı Parmenides* [Istanbul: İşaret Yayınları, 1989]: 201).

46. Ali Bulaç, "Ahlaki ve fikri iki sapma," *Kitap Dergisi,* nos. 16–17 (June–July 1988): 22.

47. Emine Şenlikoğlu, *Bize Nasıl Kıydınız* (Istanbul: Mektup Yayınları, n.d.), 227–70.

48. Emine Şenlikoğlu, *İslam'da Erkek* (Istanbul: Mektup Yayınları, 1988), 164.

49. "An Islamic Activist: Zaynab al-Ghazali," *Women and the Family in the Middle East: New Voices of Change,* ed. Elizabeth W. Fernea (Austin: University of Texas Press, 1985), 236.

50. Çakır, *Ayet ve Slogan,* 195–96.

51. "İslami arabeskin dili," *Kitap Dergisi,* no. 28 (June 1989).

52. Arat, "Feminizm ve İslam," 95–99.

53. For an elaboration on the suggestion that child care should be shared equally by mothers and fathers, starting at possibly earlier ages, and its positive effects on the development of a child's personality, see Nancy Chodorow, *The Reproduction of Mothering* (Berkley: University of California Press, 1974).

54. As a consequence of my research and its own interviews held with the

participants of the discussion group, the weekly magazine *Nokta* prepared a cover issue on "Veiled Feminists." See *Nokta,* no. 50 (1987).

55. Ali Bulaç, "Feminist bayanların kısa aklı," *Zaman,* 17 March 1987.

56. Mualla Gülnaz, "Ali Bulaç'ın düşündürdükleri," *Zaman,* 1 September 1987.

57. Tuba Tuncer, "Kimin aklı kısa?" *Zaman,* 1 September 1987.

58. Elif H. Toros, "Feminist kime derler?" *Zaman,* 15 September 1987.

59. Bouhdiba, *La Sexualité,* 282.

60. Fatma Kuru, "Kadın sorunu mu, kadının sorunu mu?" *Girişim* (July-August 1987).

61. These articles are published in *Zaman,* 3 September 1987.

62. Tuba Tuncer, "Kadın, yine kadındır," *Zaman,* 15 September 1987.

63. Yıldız Kavuncu, "İslam'da kadın ya da ipekböceği," *Zaman,* 29 September, 1987.

64. Mualla Gülnaz, "Biz kimiz?" *Zaman,* 15 September 1987.

65. Ali Sali, "Daraya iharet Edenler" (The Betrayers of the Struggle), (Laman, 29 September 1987).

66. Tuba Tuncer, "Kadın yine kadındır," *Zaman,* 15 September 1987.

67. Mualla Gülnaz, "Ali Bulaç'ın düşündürdükleri," *Zaman,* 1 September 1987.

68. Yıldız Kavuncu, "İslam'da kadın ya da İpekböceği," *Zaman,* 29 September 1987.

69. Tuba Tuncer, "Kadınlar, yine kadındır," *Zaman,* 15 September 1987.

70. Halime Toros (interview), "Siperlerimize çekildik," *Nokta,* no. 88, 17 February 1991.

71. Halime Toros, *Tanımsız* (Istanbul: Damla Neşriyat, 1990), 95–96.

72. Malek Chebel, *L'Esprit de Sérail* (Paris: Lieu Commun, 1988), 120.

73. Mualla Gülnaz, "Biz kimiz ?" *Zaman,* 15 September 1987.

CHAPTER 5

1. The "civilized society" (civil society) concept of Hegel determines the characteristics of the modern West European civilization, and it basically refers to institutionalization and moral reality, which rest upon the right of property and organizations which, for the first time, identify themselves with the public and operate independently of the central government. Şerif Mardin, *Din ve İdeoloji* (1969; reprint, Istanbul: İletişim Yayınları, 1983), 85–86.

2. Pierre Bourdieu, *Esquisse d'une théorie de la pratique: précédée de trois études d'ethnologie kabyle* (Geneva: Droz, 1972), 94.

3. For an elaborative analysis of the concept of the "invention of tradition," see Eric Hobsbawm and Terence Ranger, *The Invention of Tradition* (Cambridge: Cambridge University Press, 1983).

4. Mardin argues that "low-brow" culture remained stagnant in Turkey because of the fact that the state was ahead of the social groups, which could

have developed local themes. Thus, one does not find any Ottoman Beethoven or Schubert whose concerns were with rural themes; in the West the novel and music were nourished by low-brow culture (Mardin, *Din ve İdeoloji*, 97).

5. Mardin, "Türkiye'de muhalefet ve kontrol, "*Türk Modernleşmesi*," 186.

6. For an analysis of the fall of public men who are defined by their social roles, see Richard Sennett, *The Fall of Public Man* (New York: Vintage Books, 1978).

7. For a critical analysis of the explosion of "private life," see Nurdan Gürbilek, "Mahrumiyet," *Defter*, no. 16 (April–July 1991).

8. Lipovestky acknowledges the constant overlapping of the private and public spheres. Using examples from the feminist movement's abortion and antirape campaigns, he claims that protest movements indeed reinforce this process (Lipovestky, *L'Ère du vide: essais sur l'individualisme contemporain* [Paris: Gallimard, 1983]).

9. Foucault, *History of Sexuality*.

10. Ibid.

11. Paul Yonnet, *Jeux, modes et masses* (Paris: Gallimard, 1985), 93–140.

12. For an elaboration on the visual and sexual privileges in the literature of postmodern culture and feminism, see Craig Owens, "The Discourse of Others: Feminists and Postmodernism," in *Postmodern Culture*, ed. Hal Foster (London: Pluto Press, 1985), 70.

13. Nükhet Sirman-Eralp discerned essentialist definitions within the Islamic women's movement (Sirman-Eralp, "Feminism in Turkey: A Short History," *New Perspectives on Turkey* 3, no. 1 (Fall 1989): 1–34.

14. Arlene Elowe Macleod, *Accommodating Protest: Working Women and the New Veiling and Change in Cairo* (Cairo: University of Cairo Press, 1991).

15. It is even the case that the Islamic movement directly referred to the Western counterculture and claimed that 1968's slogan, formulated by French youth, "Be realistic and ask for the impossible," seems relevant to the demands of young Muslims as well (Hüseyin Öcal and Kemal Öztürk, "İslamcı hareket ve gençlik," *Girişim*, no. 58 [July 1990]. See also "İslami harekette aydın ve ulema," *Girişim*, no. 57 [June 1990]; and "Türkiye'de İslami hareket," *Girişim*, no. 54 [March 1990]).

16. As pointed out by Kepel in his fine analysis of the Islamic movements in France, "Islamization" is related to social participation and the administration of modernity (Kepel, *Les Banlieues de l'İslam* [Paris: Seuil, 1987]).

17. Mardin, *Din ve İdeoloji*, 122.

18. Ibid., 58.

19. Benedict Anderson, *Imagined Communities: Reflections on the Origin and Spread of Nationalism* (Thetford: Thetford Press, 1983), 15-16.

20. The alliance established prior to the general elections in October 1992 between the nationalist and the Islamic parties (the Nationalist Working Party and the Welfare Party, respectively), for example, supports this claim.

21. Mohammed Arkoun, *Pour une critique de la raison islamique* (Paris: Maisonneuve et Larose, 1984).

22. Şerif Mardin uses the concept of "opportunity realm" as "the totality of a sphere one can use to improve or increase his/her economic status" (Mardin, "Türkiye: Bir ekonomik kodun dönüşümü," *Türk Modernleşmesi*, 205. Here I refer to the participation of women in education and politics. It is Yeşim Arat who used the term for the first time in relation to women (Arat, "1980'ler Türkiye'sinde Kadın Hareketi: Liberal feminizmin radikal uzantısı," Toplum ve Bilim [1991]).

Bibliography

Abadan-Unat, Nermin. "Toplumsal değişme ve Türk kadını." In *Türk Toplumunda Kadın*, ed. N. Abadan-Unat. Ankara: Türk Sosyal Bilimler Derneği Yayınları, 1982.

Abu-Lughod, Lila. *Veiled Sentiments: Honor and Poetry in a Bedouin Society.* Berkeley; University of California Press, 1986.

Acar, Feride. "Türkiye'de İslamcı Hareket ve kadın." In *Kadın Bakış Açısından 1980'ler Türkiye'sinde Kadın*, ed. Şirin Tekeli. Istanbul: İletişim Yayınları, 1990.

Anderson, Benedict. *Imagined Communities: Reflections on the Origin and Spread of Nationalism.* Thetford: Thetford Press, 1983.

Adıvar, Halide Edip. *Yeni Turan*, 1912. Reprint. Atlas Kitabevi, 1982.

———. *Raik' in Annesi.* 1912. Reprint. Atlas Kitabevi, 1990.

Ağaoğlu, Süreyya. *Bir Ömür Böyle Geçti.* Ağaoğlu Yayınları, 1984.

Ahano, Marcel. "Le Politologue et l'hystérique," *CEMOTI*, no. 10 (1990).

Ahmed, Leila. *Women and Gender in Islam.* New Haven: Yale University Press, 1992.

Aktaş, Cihan. *Kılık, Kıyafet ve İktidar*, vol. 1. Istanbul: Nehir Yayınları, 1989.

———. *Tesettür ve Toplum: Başörtülü Öğrencilerin Toplumsal Kökeni Üzerine Bir İnceleme.* Istanbul: Nehir Yayınları, 1991.

Al-Ghazali, Zaynab. "An Islamic Activist: Zaynab al-Ghazali." In *Women and the Family in the Middle East: New Voices of Change*, ed. E. W. Fernea. Austin: University of Texas Press, 1985.

Alkan, Mehmet Ö. "Tanzimat'tan sonra kadın'ın hukuksal statüsü." *Toplum ve Bilim*, no. 50 (Summer 1990).

Anderson, Benedict. *Imagined Communities: Reflections on the Origin and Spread of Nationalism.* Thetford: Thetford Press, 1983.

Arat, Yeşim. *The Patriarchal Paradox: Women Politicians in Turkey.* London and Toronto: Associated University Presses, 1989.

———. "Feminizm and Islam: Kadın ve Aile Dergisi'nin düşündürdükleri." In *Kadın Bakış Açısından 1980'ler Türkiye'sinde Kadın*, ed. Şirin Tekeli. Istanbul: İletişim Yayınları, 1990.

———. "1980'ler Türkiye'sinde Kadın Hareketi: Liberal Kemalizm'in Radikal Uzantısı?" *Toplum ve Bilim* (1991).

Arkoun, Mohammed. *Pour une critique de la raison islamique.* Paris: Maisonneuve et Larose, 1984.

Arsel, Ilhan, *Şeriat ve Kadın*. Istanbul: Orhanlar Matbaası, 1987.

Asim, Salahaddin. *Türk Kadınlığının Tereddisi yahud Karılaşmak*, new ed. *Osmanlıda Kadınlığın Durumu*. Istanbul: Arba Yayınları, 1989.

Atatürk'ün Söylev ve Demeçleri. Konya Kadınları ile Konuşma, 21 March 1923.

Avci, Nabi. *Bombacı Parmenides*. Istanbul: İsaret Yayınları, 1989.

———. Interview (Necati Polat). *Gergadan*, no. 11 (January 1988).

Ayubi, Nazih. *Political Islam: Religion and Politics in the Arab World*. London and New York: Routledge, 1991.

Al-Azmeh, Aziz. *Islams and Modernities*. London: Verso, 1993.

Bauman, Zygmunt. *Legislators and Interpreters: On Modernity, Post-Modernity and Intellectuals*. Ithaca: Cornell University Press, 1987.

Beck, Louis, and Nikki Keddie, eds. *Women in the Muslim World*. Cambridge, Mass.: Harvard University Press, 1978.

Berkes, Niyazi. *Türkiye'de Çağdaşlaşma*. Ankara: Bilgi Yayınevi, 1973.

Berktay, Fatma. "Türkiye solunun kadına bakışı: değişen bir şey var mı?" *Kadın In Bakiş Açısından 1980'ler Türkiye'sinde Kadın*, ed. Şirin Tekeli. Istanbul: İletişim Yayınları, 1990.

Bouhdiba, Abdelwahab. *La sexualité en Islam*. Quadrige, Paris: Presses Universitaire de France, 1975.

Bourdieu, Pierre. *Esquisse d'une théorie de la pratique, précédée de trois études d'ethnologie kablye*. Geneva: Droz, 1972.

———. *La Distinction, critique sociale du jugement*. Paris: Editions du Minuit, 1979. (Published in English as *Distinction*. Cambridge, Mass.: Harvard University Press, 1984.)

Bulaç, Ali. *İslam Dünyasında Düşünce Sorunları*, Istanbul: İnsan Yayınları, 1985.

———. "Feminist bayanların kısa aklı." *Zaman*, 17 March 1985.

———. "Ahlaki ve fikri iki sapma." *Kitap Dergisi*, nos. 16–17, June-July 1988.

———. *Din ve Modernizm*. Istanbul: Endülüs Yayınları, 1990.

Çakir, Ruşen. *Ayet ve Slogan*. Istanbul: Metis Yayınları, 1990.

Çalişlar, Oral. *İslam'da Kadın ve Cinsellik*. Istanbul: Afa Yayınları, 1991.

Caporal, Bernard. *Kemalizmde ve Kemalizm Sonrasında Türk Kadını*. Ankara: İş Bankası Kültür Yayınları, 1982.

Chebel, Malek. *L'Esprit de Sérail*. Paris: Lieu Commun, 1982.

Chodorow, Nancy. *The Reproduction of Mothering*. Berkley: University of California Press, 1974.

Desmet-Gregoire, Hélène. "De la perception d'une femme ottomane à celle des femmes ottomanes: le récit de voyage d'une europénne du XIXe siècle. La princesse de Belgiojoso." *Contributions à l'histoire économique et sociale de l'Empire Ottomane*. Louvain: Peeters, 1983.

Develioğlu, Ferit. *Osmanlıca-Türkçe Ansiklopedik Lugat*. Ankara: Doğuş Matbaası, 1970.

Djait, H. "Dimensions l'orientalisme islamisant." *Le Mal de voir*. Paris: Union Générale d'Editions. (10/18, Cahier Jussieu).

Duben, Alan, and Cem Behar. *Istanbul Households: Marriage, Family and Fertility, 1880–1940*. Cambridge: Cambridge University Press, 1991.

Dumont, Paul. *Mustafa Kemal*. Paris: Complexe, 1983.
Durakbaşa, Ayşe. *The Formation of "Kemalist Female Identity": A Historical Cultural Perspective*. Master's thesis, Department of Sociology, Boğaziçi University, 1987.
———. "Cumhuriyet döneminde Kemalist kadın kimliğinin oluşumu." *Tarih ve Toplum* 9, no. 52 (1988): 167–71.
El-Guindi, Fatwa. "Veiled Activism: Egyptian Women in the Contemporary Islamic Movement." *Peuples Méditerranéens*, nos. 22–23 (1983): 79–90.
Elias, Norbert. *The History of Manners: The Civilizing Process*, vol. 1. New York: Pantheon Books, 1978.
Engınün, Inci. *Halide Edip Adıvar'ın Eserlerinde Doğu-Batı Meselesi*. Istanbul:Edebiyat Fakültesi Matbaası, 1978.
Etienne, Bruno. *L'Islamisme radical*. Paris: Hachette, 1987.
Farrere, Claude. *Türklerin Manevi Gücü*. Istanbul: Tercüman 1001 Temel Eser. (Originally published as *Extraordinaire aventure d'Ahmet Pasha Dj, maleddine*. Paris: Ernest Flammarion, 1921.)
Foucault, Michel. *L'usage des plaisirs: histoire de la sexualité*, vol. 2. Paris: Gallimard, 1984. (Published in English as *The History of Sexuality*, vol. 1, trans. Robert Hurley. New York: Vintage Books, 1990.
Georgeon, François, *Türk Milliyetçiliğinin Kökenleri: Yusuf Akçura*. Ankara: Yurt Yayınları, 1986.
Giddens, Anthony. *Modernity and Self-Identity: Self and Society in the Late Modern Age*. Stanford: Stanford University Press, 1991.
Göçek, Fatma Müge. *East Encounters West: France and the Ottoman Empire in the Eighteenth Century*. Oxford University Press, New York: 1987.
Gökalp, Ziya. *Türkçülüğün Esasları: Kültür Bakanlığı Yayınları*. Istanbul: Milli Eğitim Basımevi, 1976.
———. *Türkleşmek, Islamlaşmak, Muasırlaşmak*. Ankara: Kültür Bakanlığı Yayınları, 1976.
———. *Limmi ve Malta Mektupları*. Ed. F. A. Tansel. Ankara: Türk Tarih Kurumu Yayınları, 1985.
Göle, Nilüfer. "Ingénieurs musulmans et étudiantes voilées en Turquie: entre le totalitarisme et l'individualisme." In *Intellectuels et militants de d'islam contemporain*, ed. Gille Kepel and Yann Richard. Paris: Seuil, 1990.
———. *Musulmanes et Modernes: voile et civilisation en Turquie*. Paris: Editions de la Découverte, 1993.
Göloğlu, Mahmut. *Devrimler ve Tepkileri, 1924–1930*. Ankara: Başnur Matbaası, 1972.
Graham-Brown, Sarah. *Images of Women: The Portrayal of Women in Photography of the Middle East, 1860–1950*. New York: Columbia University Press, 1988.
Gülnaz, Mualla. "Ali Bulaç'ın Düşündürdükleri." *Zaman*, 1 September 1987.
———. "Biz Kimiz?" *Zaman*, 15 September 1987.
Gürbılek, Nurdan. "Mahrumiyet." *Defter*, no. 16 (April-July 1991).
Güzel, M. Şehmuz. "1908 kadınları." *Tarih ve Toplum* 1, no. 7 (1984).
Hatemı, Hüseyin. *Kadının Çıkış Yolu*. Ankara: Fecr Yayınevi, 1988.

Hobsbawm, Eric, and Terrance Ranger. *The Invention of Tradition.* Cambridge: Cambridge University Press, 1983.

Ibrahim, Saadeddin. "Anatomy of Egypt's Militant Islamic Groups." *International Journal of Middle East Studies* (1980): 423–53.

Işın, Ekrem. "Tanzimat, kadın ve gündelik hayat." *Tarih ve Toplum* 9, no. 51 (1988): 150–55.

Jackh, Ernest. *Yükselen Hilal.* Uğur Kitabevi, 1946.

Kandıyotı, Deniz. "Ataerkil örüntüler: Türk toplumunda erkek egemenliğinin çözümlenmesine yönelik notlar." In *Kadın Bakış Açısından 1980'ler Türkiye'sinde Kadın,* ed. Şirin Tekeli. Istanbul: İletişim Yayınları, 1990.

Kara, Ismail. *Türkiye'de Islamcılık Düşüncesi I.* Istanbul: Risale Yayınları, 1986.

———. Interview (Mehmet Metiner). *Girişim,* May 1987.

———. Interview (Sefa Kaplan). *Nokta,* 31 December 1989.

———. "Islamcılar, mucizeler, bilim ve pozitivizm." *Dergah,* no. 6 (August 1990): 18–19.

Karaosmanoğlu, Yakup Kadri. *Ankara.* Istanbul: İletişim Yayınları, 1934.

Kavuncu, Yıldız. "Islam'da kadın ya da ipekböceği", *Zaman,* 15 September 1987.

Kepel, Gilles. *Les Banlieues de l'Islam.* Paris: Seuil, 1987.

———. *La Revanche de Dieu.* Paris: Seuil, 1991.

Küçükömer, Idris. *Düzenin Yabancılaşması.* 1969. Reprint. Istanbul: Alan Yayınları, 1989.

Kudret, Cevdet. "Alafranga dedikleri." *Tarih ve Toplum* 1, no. 4 (1984): 267–68.

Kuru, Fatma. "Kadın sorunu mu, kadının sorunu mu?" *Girişim* (July-August 1987).

Leonardo, Micaela di. *Gender at the Crossroads of Knowledge: Feminist Anthropology in the Postmodern Era.* Berkeley: University of California Press, 1991.

Lerner, Daniel. *The Passing of Traditional Society: Modernizing the Middle East.* New York: The Free Press, 1958.

Lewis, Bernard. *The Emergence of Modern Turkey.* London: Oxford University Press, 1968.

———. "Islamic Political Movements." *Middle East Review* (Summer 1985).

Macleod, Arlene Elowe. *Accommodating Protest: Working Women and the New Veiling in Cairo.* Ph.D. diss., Yale University, 1987.

Mannheim, Karl. *Ideology and Utopia.* New York: Harvest Books, 1936.

Mardın, Şerif. *Din ve Ideoloji.* Istanbul: İletişim Yayınları, 1983.

———. *Türkiye'de Toplum ve Siyaset.* Istanbul: İletişim Yayınları, 1990.

———. "Super Westernization in the Ottoman Empire in the Last Quarter of the Nineteenth Century." In *Turkey: Geographic and Social Perspectives,* ed. P. Benedict et al. Leiden: E. J. Brill, 1974.

Mernissi, Fatima. *Le Harem politique.* Paris: Albin Michel, 1987.

———. *Beyond the Veil.* 1985. Reprint. Bloomington and Indianapolis: Indiana University Press, 1987.

Mert, Nuray. *A Study on the Change of Ottoman Clothing Habits.* Thesis, Department of History, Boğaziçi University, 1983.

Mills, C. Wright. *The Sociological Imagination.* New York: Penguin Books, 1971.

Milani, Farzaneh. *Veils and Words: The Emerging Voices of Iranian Women Writers.* Syracuse: Syracuse University Press, 1992.

Moran, Berna. *Türk Romanına Eleştirel Bir Bakış 1.* 1983. Reprint. Istanbul: İletişim Yayınları, 1990.

Nieuwenhuijze, C. A. O. Van. *The Lifestyles of Islam.* Leiden: E. J. Brill, 1985.

Olson, Emelie A. "Muslim Identity and Secularism in Contemporary Turkey: The Headscarf Dispute." *Anthropological Quarterly* 58, no. 6 (October 1985).

Owens, Craig. "The Discourse of Others: Feminists and Post-Modernism." In *Postmodern Culture,* ed. H. Foster. London: Pluto Press, 1985.

"Osmanlı Yaşayışıyla Ilgili Belgeler: Kadın-I." *Tarih ve Toplum* 1, no. 3 (1984): 192-99.

"Osmanlı Yaşayışıyla Ilgili Belgeler: Kadın-II." *Tarih ve Toplum* 1, no. 3 (1984): 289-96.

Özankaya, Özer. "Laiklik öncesi dönemde Şemseddin Sami'nin aile düzenine ilişkin görüşleri." *Türkiye'de Ailenin Değişimi.* Türk Sosyal Bilimler Derneği, 1984.

Özbay, Ferhunde. "Development of Studies on Women in Turkey." *The Study of Women in Turkey: An Anthology,* ed. Ferhunde Özbay. Report of UNESCO and the Association of Turkish Social Sciences, 1986.

Özel, Ismet *Waldo Sen Nerde Burda Değilsin?* Istanbul: Risale Yayınları, 1988.

Parla, Jale. *Babalar ve Oğullar: Tanzimat Romanının Epistemolojik Temelleri.* Istanbul: İletişim Yayınları, 1990.

Parla, Taha. *Ziya Gökalp, Kemalizm ve Türkiye'de Korporatizm.* Istanbul: İletişim Yayınları, 1989.

Ricoeur, Paul. "L'Histoire comme recit et comme pratique." *Espirit,* no. 6 (June 1989).

Rugh, Andrea B. *Reveal and Conceal: Dress in Contemporary Egypt.* Syracuse: Syracuse University Press, 1986.

Safa, Peyami. *Türk İnkilābına Bakışlar.* 1938. Reprint. Kanaat Kitabevi: Ankara Kütüphanesi Tarih Serisi, 1959.

Said, Edward. *Orientalism.* New York: Pantheon, 1978.

Said Halım Paşa. *Buhranlarımız.* 1919. Reprint. Istanbul: Tercüman 1001 Eser, n.d.

Shayegan, Daryush. *Le Regard mutile.* Paris: Albin Michel, 1989.

Shils, Edward. "Centre and Periphery," *The Logic of Personal Knowledge: Essays Presented to Michael Polanyi.* London: Routledge and Kegan Paul, 1961.

Simmel, Georg. *Philosophie de la modernité: la femme, la ville, l'individualisme.* 1923. Reprint. Paris: Editions Payot, 1989.

Somers, Margaret G., and Gloria D. Gibson. "Reclaiming the Epistemological 'Other': Narrative and the Social Constitution of Identity." In *Social Theory and the Politics of Identity,* ed. Craig Calhoun. Cambridge, Mass.: Blackwell, 1994.

Stowasser, Barbara F. *Women in the Qur'an, Traditions, and Interpretation.* Oxford: Oxford University Press, 1994.

Sunar, Ilkay. *Düşün ve Toplum*. 1979. Reprint. Ankara: Birey ve Toplum Yayınları, 1986.

Şaylan, Gencay. "Genç Müslümanlar ve Islamcı Hareket." *Cumhuriyet*, 18–23 March 1990.

Şeni, Nora. "Ville Ottomane et représentations du corps féminin." *Les Temps modernes (Turkey)*, nos. 456–57 (July-August 1984).

———. "19. yüzyıl sonu Istanbul basınında moda ve kadın kıyafetleri." In *Kadın Bakış Açısından 1980'ler Türkiye'sinde Kadın*, ed. Şirin Tekeli. Istanbul: Iletişim Yayınları, 1990.

Şenlıkoğlu, Emine. *Bize Nasıl Kıydınız?* Istanbul: Mektup Yayınları, n.d.

———. *Islam'da Erkek*. Istanbul: Mektup Yayınları, 1988.

Taylor, Charles. *Multiculturalism: Examining the Politics of Recognition*, Intro. and ed. Amy Gutman. Princeton: Princeton University Press, 1994.

Tanpinar, Ahmed Hamdi. *Yaşadığım Gibi*. Istanbul: Dergāh Yayınları, n.d.

Taşçıoğlu, Muhaddere. *Türk Osmanlı Cemiyetinde Kadının Sosyal Durumu ve Kadın Kıyafetleri*. Ankara: Akın Matbaası, 1958.

Taşkıran, Tezer. *Cumhuriyet'in 50. Yılında Türk Kadın Hakları*. Başbakanlık Basımevi: Başbakanlık Kültür Müşteşarliği, 1973.

Tekelı, Şırır. *Kadınlar ve Siyasal Toplumsal Hayat*. Istanbul: Birikim Yayıları, 1982.

———. "Türkiye'de kadının siyasal hayattaki yeri." In *Türk Toplumunda Kadın*, ed. Nermin Abadan Unat. 1979. Reprint. Istanbul: Sosyal Bilimler Araştırma Dizisi, Ekin Yayınları, 1982.

———. "The Meaning and the Limits of Feminist Ideology in Turkey." In *The Study of Women in Turkey: An Anthology*, ed. Ferhunde Özbay. Report. Paris: UNESCO and the Association of Turkish Social Sciences, 1986.

Tillion, Germaine. *Le Harem et les cousins*. Paris: Seuil, 1966.

Tocqueville, Alexis de. *De la démocratie en Amérique I*. Paris: Garnier-Flammarion, 1981.

Toprak, Binnaz. "Türk toplumunda kadın." In *Türk Kadını ve Din*, ed. Nermin Abadan Unat. Ankara: Türk Sosyal Bilimler Derneği, 1979.

———. "Women and Fundamentalism: The Case of Turkey." Paper presented at the Round Table on Identity Politics and Woman, Helsinki, 1990.

Toprak, Zafer. "Kadınlar Halk Fırkası." *Tarih ve Toplum* 9, no. 51 (1989): 158–59.

———. "Kadın askerler ve milli aile." *Tarih ve Toplum* 9, no. 51 (1989): 162–66.

———. "Meşrutiyet yıllarında kadınlara dair söylenmiş sözler." *Tarih ve Toplum* 9, no. 51 (1988): 174.

———. "Politics, Women and Family during the Second Constitutional Period." Paper presented at The Turkish Family and Domestic Organization, New York, 23–25 April 1986.

Toros, Elif H. "Feminist kime derler?" *Zaman*, 15 September 1987.

Toros, Halime. Interview. "Siperlerimize çekildik." *Nokta*, no. 88 (17 February 1991).

———. *Tanımsız*. Istanbul: Damla Neşriyat, 1990.

Touraine, Alain. *Production de la société*. Paris: Editions du Seuil, 1973. (Published in English as *The Self-Production of Society*, trans. Derek Coltman. Chicago: University of Chicago Press, 1977.)

———. *La Voix et le regard*. Paris: Editions du Seuil, 1978. (Published in English as *The Voice and the Eye: An Analysis of Social Movement*. Cambridge: Cambridge University Press, 1981.)

Tozduman, Aysel Z. *Islam'da Kadın Hakları: Kadın ve Aile* (Ankara: 1988).

Tuğlacı, Pars. *Osmanlı Saray Kadınları*. Istanbul: Cem Yayınevi, 1985.

Tuman, Hatice. "Çiçekler rahmetle büyür." *Mektup* 3, no. 31 (August 1987): 27.

Tunaya, Tarık Zafer. *Türkiye'nin Siyasi Hayatında Batılılaşma Hareketleri*. Istanbul: Yedigün Matbaası, 1960.

———. *Islamcılık Cereyanı*. Istanbul, 1962.

———. "Milli Rönesans." *Tarih ve Toplums* (1986).

Tuncer, Tuba. "Kimin aklı kısa?" *Zaman*, 1 September 1987.

———. "Kadınlar yine kadındır." *Zaman*, 15 September 1987.

Tımur, Taner. *Osmanlı Kimliği*. Istanbul: Hil Yayınları, 1986.

Ücken, Hilmi Ziya. *Türkiye'de Çağdaş Düşünce Tarihi*. 1966. Reprint. Istanbul: Üljen Yayınları, 1979.

Yavuz, Hilmi. *Kültür Üzerine*. Istanbul: Bağlam Yayınları, 1987.

———. *Roman Kavramı ve Türk Romanı*. Ankara: Bilgi Yayınevi, 1977.

Zuhur, Sherifa. *Revealing Reveiling: Islamist Gender Ideology in Contemporary Egypt*. New York: State University of New York Press, 1992.

Index

alaturka (*alla turca*, Turkish), 15 16
  Kemalist reaction and, 65
alla franca (European), 15, 60
Ankara, 69

Beauty, definition of, 66–67
Body, 135–37
  female, and Western civilization,
    137
  Islamic, 136
  physical fitness and, 135–36
  as symbol of resistance, 135

Civil law, 74–77
  Kemalism and, 74
  modernization and, 76
  nationalism and, 76
  Sharia and, 75
Civilization
  a cultivated person and, 59
  culture and, 58–59
  definition of, 12–13, 45
  magic and, 46–47
  material and spiritual aspects of, 31
  modernization and, 13, 31
  nationalist ideology and, 62–63
  power relations and, 15
  superiority of the West and, 13,
    58
  Turkish society and, 47
  universalism and, 13
  Westernist perspective of, 37
Civilization project, 32, 134
Constitutional Period (1908–1919),
    (Constitutional Monarchy) 36–56

  ideal of progress during, 36
  Islamization and, 36
  women and, 36–37
  reform efforts during, 36
Culture, 58–59. *See also* Turkish cul-
    ture

Democracy
  in early Turkish society, 47
  equality and, 52
Difference
  as concern of Islamists, 95
  as context of identity politics, 17
  as empowerment, 17
  in Islamism, 112
  as mirror image of equality, 137
Dualism
  between civilization and culture,
    61–62
  between civilization and tradition,
    68–69
  in Turkish history, 57–58

Education, 95–98
  impact of Kemalist reforms, 73
  Islamist legitimation of, 103
  Islamist traditionalists and, 43
  Islamist women and, 114–16
  life strategies and, 114
  motherhood and, 32, 99
  professional identity and, 115
  purposes of, 116
  required by Islam, 96–97
  veiling and, 84, 92
  work and, 99–102

Equality
civil law and, 76 n58
collective consciousness and, 106–7
democratic societies and, 137
Western societies' development
and, 51–52
progress and, 77
in Golden Age of Islam, 104
the Koran and, 105
modernization and, 39
as problematic for Islamists, 18
universalism and, 138
work and, 101

Family, 57
as experienced reality, 119–21
in Golden Age of Islam, 119–20
women's inequality and, 106
Fashion and manners, 61, 67
in urban and public spaces, 134–
35
Kemalist reforms and, 58
moral function of, 93
as political statement, 85
semiotics of body care and, 18
state regulation of, 48–49, 72
styles of dress and, 59–61, 66–67
as transcultural and transclass,
134
Western civilization and, 67
Feminism, 121–27, 138
during Constitutional Period,
49–50
in early Turkish society, 47
equality and, 138
Islamist critique of, 122
Islamist women and, 122–24, 128
Kemalist ideology and, 81
leftist ideologies and, 81
need for, 121–22
Young Turks and, 50
See also Turkish culture
Feminism, Kemalist, 71–74, 79–82
feminist critique of, 81–82
participation of women and, 79
Freedom, 43

Golden Age of Islam, 104–8, 119
cultural Islam and, 111
equality and, 104
Islamist social projects and, 107
as Islamist utopia, 103, 104
modernization and, 34
women and, 119, 128
traditional Islam and, 104

habitus, 16, 132
"Headscarf dispute," 5
Historicity, 9, 18, 28 n15
Historicity, weak
as analogous to development lag, 12
definition of, 28 n5
disassociation between elites and
people and, 133
modernization and, 51
in relation to West, 28
Humanism, 40

Identity
Islamist, 20–21
of Islamist women, 126, 128, 129
of Kemalist women, 78
national, 44, 134
sexual, 43–44, 79
women's domestic rules and, 104–5
Iran, 109
Iranian Revolution, 83–84
Islam
captivity of women and, 86
as ideology, 86
increasing strength in Turkey, 88
misinterpretations of, 32–33
modern society and, 138–39
nationalism and, 139
sexuality and, 93
social change and, 96
Turkish modernization and, 97
Turkist movement and, 46
Western civilization and, 41
Islam, cultural, 108–10
Islam, political, 108–30
gender identity and, 112, 113
gender relations and, 113